WRIGHTSLAW

All About IEPs

Answers to Frequently Asked Questions About IEPs

Peter W. D. Wright, Esq.
Pamela Darr Wright, MA, MSW
Sandra Webb O'Connor, M.Ed.

Harbor House Law Press, Inc.
Hartfield, Virginia 23071

Wrightslaw: All About IEPs
by Peter W. D. Wright, Pamela Darr Wright and Sandra Webb O'Connor

Library of Congress Cataloging-in-Publication Data
Wright, Peter W. D., Pamela Darr Wright and Sandra Webb O'Connor
Wrightslaw: All About IEPs.
p. cm.
Includes bibliographic references and index.
ISBN 13: 978-1-892320-20-9
1. Education — Parenting — United States. I. Title
2. Special education — parent participation — United States.
Library of Congress Control Number: 2009906167

Printed in the United States of America.
10 9 8 7 6 5 4 3

Printing History
Harbor House Law Press, Inc. issues new printings and new editions to keep our publications current. New printings include technical corrections and minor changes. New editions include major revisions of text and/or changes.
First Edition: January 2010 Third Printing: October 2010

Disclaimer
The purpose of this book is to educate and inform. While every effort has been made to make this book as accurate as possible, there may be mistakes, both typographical and in content. The authors and Harbor House Law Press, Inc. shall have neither liability nor responsibility to any person or entity with respect to loss or damage caused, or alleged to be caused, directly or indirectly, by the information contained in this book. If you do not wish to be bound by the above, you may return the book to the publisher for a full refund. Every effort has been made to ensure that no copyrighted material has been used without permission. The authors regret any oversights that may have occurred and are happy to rectify them in future printings of this book.

When You Use a Self-Help Book
Law is always changing. The information contained in this book is general information and may or may not reflect current legal developments. This book is designed to provide general information in regard to the subject matter covered. It is sold with the understanding that the publisher and authors are not engaged in rendering legal or other professional services. For legal advice about a specific set of facts, you should consult with an attorney.

Bulk Purchases
Harbor House Law Press books are available at half price discounts for bulk purchases, academic sales or textbook adoptions. For information, contact Harbor House Law Press, P. O. Box 480, Hartfield VA 23071. Please provide the title of the book, ISBN number, quantity, how the book will be used, and date needed. Toll Free Phone Orders: (877) LAW IDEA or (877) 529-4332. Toll Free Fax Orders: (800) 863-5348. Internet Orders: orders@ harborhouselaw.com

Acknowledgements

We thank the thousands of parents, teachers, service providers, and advocates who have asked questions and shared concerns educating children with disabilities. We are grateful for these courageous people whose determination to solve special education problems continues to inspire us.

We wish to acknowledge the contributions of several individuals who provided ideas for this book.

Kayla Bower, Director of thc Oklahoma Disability Law Center, proposed that we write this book years ago.

Susan Bruce, Parent Advocate and Parent Education Coordinator, PRO*Parents of SC, provided excellent advice about measurable IEP goals, accommodations and modifications, transition, and diploma options.

Pam Cook, Special Education Consultant and Advocate from Pittsburg, offered invaluable information about measurable IEP goals, progress monitoring, assistive technology, and Universal Design for Learning.

Jackie Igafo-Te'o, parent of two children with disabilities, and website/data consultant for disability-related organizations, provided excellent information about educating children with behavior disorders, functional behavior assessments, and positive behavior intervention plans.

We owe a special debt of gratitude to ***Patty Roberts***, Clinical Assistant Professor of Law and Director, PELE Special Education Advocacy Clinic, William & Mary Law School, and to ***Jeff Martin***, parent of a child with a disability and law student in the PELE Special Education Advocacy Clinic at William & Mary Law School. Patty and Jeff edited the rough draft of the entire manuscript, and offered many suggestions that we included in the book.

Many people selflessly poured their time and energy into ***Wrightslaw: All About IEPs***. We want to acknowledge and thank you for reading and critiquing sections of the manuscript.

Jennifer Bacon, Family Advocate, PELE Special Education Advocacy Clinic, William & Mary Law School, Williamsburg, Virginia

Sam and Dina Baugh, Parent Advocates for a child with cerebral palsy, California

Betsy Moog Brooks, The Moog Center for Deaf Education, St. Louis, Missouri

Marialena Casciotta, Director of Pupil Services, East Stroudsburg, Pennsylvania

Daniel J. Cavallini, Ed.D., Special Education Tutor, Career & Technology Magnet, Indianapolis Public Schools, Indiana

David Cockrell, Parent Advocate, West Columbia, South Carolina

Steven C. Freeman and Kathy Fierros Freeman, Parent Advocates, Tucson, Arizona

Mary Beth Gustafson, Ed.D., Assistant Superintendent for Special Education, Pocono Mountain School District, Pennsylvania

Debbie Harrison, Public School Teacher, Virginia

Diane Haverty, Parent Advocate, Woburn, Massachusetts

Ruth C. Heitin, Ph.D., Educational Consultant, Alexandria, Virginia

Jeanne Hollabaugh, Parent Board Member, Hands & Voices, Arizona

Rosabelle Holmes, Intensive In-Home Counselor, Youth and Prevention Division, Piedmont Community Services, Martinsville, Virginia

Blair Hornstine, Third year law student and PELE Special Education Advocacy Clinic student at William & Mary Law School, Williamsburg, Virginia

Patty Kishi, Parent Advocate and Vice-President, Autism Bridges Maui, Hawai'i

Debbie Larson, Parent Advocate, Batavia, New York

Becky McGee, Parent of a Child with a Learning Disability, Yorktown, Virginia

Elizabeth Mueller, Librarian and Parent Advocate, Tampa, Florida

Lisa Nagy and Frans Tax, Parent Advocates, Tucson, Arizona

Kiele Pennington, Parent Advocate and President of Autism Bridges Maui, Hawai'i

Sandy Pope, Parent Advocate, Fishers, Indiana

Christine A. Preston, Special Education Teacher, East Stroudsburg Area SD, East Stroudsburg, Pennsylvania

Sue Nelson Sargeant, Public School Speech Therapist and Parent Advocate, Virginia

Dr. Gina R. Scala, Chair, Special Education/Rehabilitation Department, East Stroudsburg University, Pennsylvania

Kim Stevens, Director of Pupil Services, East Stroudsburg Area SD, East Stroudsburg, Pennsylvania

Joyce Tiner, Parent of a Child with Special Needs, Hutto, Texas

Tanya Torrijos, Speech-Language Pathologist, Powhatan County Public Schools, Virginia

Suzanne Whitney, co-author of ***Wrightslaw: No Child Left Behind*** and Special Education Advocate, New Hampshire

Dedication

This book is dedicated to Pete's mentor, Robert E. Shepherd, Jr., Professor Emeritus at the University of Richmond School of Law, and advocate for troubled children. Bob Shepherd encouraged Pete to attend law school.

This book is dedicated Pam's mentor, Dr. William M. Lordi, founder of Lor-Berg Family Guidance Clinic, adjunct professor at the Medical College of Virginia, and tireless advocate for children with disabilities and their families.

This book is dedicated to Sue's parents, Joseph Earl and Viola Long Webb, to her children, Ryan and Erin, Kathryn, and Shelley, and to her grandchildren, Isabel, Evan, and Cate.

Table of Contents

Table of Questions

- May the school district bring their attorney to an IEP meeting? May we bring an attorney?
- The school board attorney attended our last. The notice we received did not include the attorney on the list of people who would attend. We felt blindsided. How should we handle this in the future?
- At the last IEP meeting, I was presented with a "draft IEP." I felt that the school made decisions about my child's special education program without input from me. Is this legal?
- Is it legal for the school to have "pre-IEP meetings" that exclude the child's parents?
- During IEP meetings, so many people talk at the same time, I can't keep track. When I get home, I can't remember what we agreed to. Can I make a recording of my child's IEP meetings so I can review them later?

3 Parental Participation & Consent

- What is my role at my child's IEP meeting?
- What should I expect in an IEP meeting?
- What is "consent?"
- As a parent, do I have to give my consent before the school can implement the IEP?
- My child has received special education services for years. I have never been asked to sign an IEP. Does the law require my signature?
- I don't agree that the proposed IEP is sufficient, but it is better than nothing. The IEP team says I have to "take it or leave it!" Can I allow the school to implement parts of the IEP while we continue to negotiate the issues where we don't agree?
- Can a foster parent or surrogate consent to the IEP?
- My daughter has made little or no progress in special education. Can I revoke consent for her to receive special education services?
- How will I know when an IEP meeting is scheduled and who will attend?
- The school says the IEP team only meets during school hours. I can't leave work during school hours but I can attend a meeting after school. Should the school comply with my request for an after-school IEP meeting?
- I want to help develop my child's IEP but I can't attend the IEP meeting. What can I do?
- I attend IEP meetings with parents who are not fluent in English. Should the school provide an interpreter so the parents know what is happening and can participate in decision-making?
- Are parents allowed to have copies of assessments and evaluations before the IEP meeting?
- Can the school have an IEP meeting without me?
- Is the school required to provide me with a copy of my child's IEP?
- When I asked for a copy of my child's IEP at the end of the meeting, the team leader said they would send me a "clean copy" later. I want a copy of the IEP we agreed upon during the meeting. What can I do?

4 Present Levels, Measurable IEP Goals, Special Education Services

- What are present levels of academic achievement and functional performance?
- Where does the IEP team get the information for present levels of academic achievement and functional performance?
- Do all IEPs include present levels of academic achievement and functional performance?
- What are "functional skills?"
- Must all IEPs include functional goals?
- Our IEP team wants to use data from two-year-old assessments for the present levels in this year's IEP. Should the IEP team use current information for the "present levels" statements?
- How can I get the IEP team to use accurate information for the present levels of achievement and performance sections of the IEP?
- I am confused about measurable goals.
- The goals in my child's IEP are not measurable: "Evan will improve in reading" and "Evan will improve in mathematics." How do you make goals measurable?
- My child has behavior problems. How do you make behavior goals measurable?
- My child's IEP has academic goals but no functional goals. Should all IEPs include functional goals?
- My child has social skills deficits but is doing fine academically. Can the IEP have goals that address her social skills deficits, but no academic goals?
- Does the IEP team have to consider my concerns about my child's special education program?
- The team says they do not write IEP goals for general education classes like pre-calculus and humanities courses. Is this correct?
- Can you give me examples of good IEP goals?
- At the last IEP meeting, the team cut my child's IEP from ten goals to four goals. Is there a legal limit to the number of goals in the IEP?
- Is the school responsible for ensuring that my child reaches all the goals in the IEP?
- My child has multiple disabilities and takes alternate assessments. Should her IEP include short-term objectives and/or benchmarks?
- Should my child's IEP include all the services he needs?
- What is peer-reviewed research?
- Should my child's IEP include specific information about the services he will receive?
- Our state wants IEP teams to develop IEPs based on state standards. I am concerned that standards-based or state aligned IEPs do not address a child's weakness in the basic skills of reading, writing, arithmetic, and spelling, and are not individualized to meet the child's needs.
- After our school changed their service delivery system, they do not specify the amount of services in IEPs. Can they do this?
- The school says my child's IEP is based on "what we have available." Is this right?

- My child has a disability and an IEP. Is she entitled to physical education?
- What is adapted physical education?
- My child has diabetes and an IEP. Can he benefit from adapted PE?

5 Related Services, Supplementary Aids & Services

- What are related services?
- What information about related services should be included in my child's IEP?
- Can a child with a disability be eligible for speech-language services, but not for special education services?
- Are there limits on the speech, physical, and occupational therapy a child can receive?
- My child was born deaf and has a cochlear implant. When I asked the school to monitor the device to ensure it is working, they said the law does not allow them to do this because the cochlear implant is a medical device. Does the law prohibit this?
- One of my students received a cochlear implant. As a teacher, what can I do to help her?
- My child has an insulin pump. Is the school responsible for maintaining or replacing this device?
- Do all children with disabilities have a right to transportation as a related service?
- My child has an orthopedic impairment and an IEP. She uses a power wheelchair. She needs ramps to get around the school and school grounds safely. Is the school required to provide transportation and assistance?
- My son has autism and an IEP. His communication skills are limited and he is easily distracted. His judgment is poor. I'm afraid to let him walk to the school bus stop. Can I ask the school to provide special transportation?
- My child has autism and an IEP. He gets overwhelmed when riding the bus. Can the bus driver get training in how to manage his behavior problems?
- My child is eligible for special education due to a traumatic brain injury. He has an aide, but still struggles in class. His teacher says he doesn't need more help, he would do fine in school if he only applied himself. Why don't teachers understand how this condition affects his ability to perform?
- My preschool child receives speech therapy at school. I would like to supplement the speech therapist's services with receptive and expressive language exercises at home. Can the school provide me with training to do this?
- My child has ADHD and has trouble completing homework. He gets frustrated and angry. I want to help him but I don't know how. Can I receive training to help my child?
- My child has an orthopedic impairment and mobility problems. The IEP team wants to eliminate mobility goals from his IEP because they do not have enough occupational and physical therapists. Do I have to let them do this?
- My child is partially paralyzed and attends mainstream classes. He requires a ventilator to breathe and a person who can attend to his physical needs at school. The school says these are medical services and they are not required to provide them. Is this correct?
- When is a child with a disability eligible for supplementary aids and services?

- Who decides what supplementary aids and services a child will receive?
- When and where should a child receive supplementary aids and services?
- Can my child's IEP include extracurricular activities and after-school programs?
- Should supplementary aids and services be listed in my child's IEP?

6 Progress, Accommodations, Modifications, & Alternate Assessments

- How will I know if my child is making progress? Is this stated in the IEP?
- Can the school district issue a report card that includes information about my child's special education program? For example, can the report card refer to my child's IEP?
- Should my child's report card assign grades based on grade level standards?
- My child's IEP states that progress will be reported by "teacher observation." I want objective information about my child's progress. Any suggestions?
- What is progress monitoring?
- Can the school use progress monitoring in the IEP?
- Since state assessments measure academic skills, how will we know if our child is making progress in developmental and functional skills?
- What is the difference between accommodations and modifications?
- My child is mainstreamed in regular classes. How can we ensure that he has the classroom accommodations he needs?
- My child has a disability and an IEP. Is he eligible for accommodations on high-stakes tests?
- Who decides if my child will take an alternate assessment?
- My child has a severe disability. Is he exempt from taking state and district assessments?
- My child was evaluated and diagnosed with dyslexia and dysgraphia. The psychologist advised that she needs a reading program based on Orton-Gillingham principles. The IEP team said the school chooses the methodology. Is this true?
- Are reading specialists required to use research based reading programs with their special education students?

7 Special Factors in IEPs

- What is a functional behavioral assessment?
- What happens in a functional behavior assessment?
- When should the IEP team refer a child for a functional behavioral assessment?
- An IEP team member observed my child in the classroom, then wrote a functional behavior assessment. Is this sufficient?
- What is a behavior intervention plan?
- My child has autism. The school had him arrested for assault. Although the charges were dismissed, I am afraid this will happen again. What can I do?
- I adopted a child from another country. His English is limited. He has a disability and an IEP. Should he receive special education in English or in his native language?
- What should be included in his IEP?

- My child has a disability and limited English. Is he entitled to services from a speech-language pathologist?
- One of my students with an IEP has very poor vision. She needs eyeglasses, but her family can't afford to purchase them. Since she cannot learn without glasses, is the school responsible for providing them?
- What does the law say about instruction in Braille?
- My child needs textbooks in Braille. Is the school responsible for ensuring that he has textbooks in Braille at the beginning of the school year?
- My child has a cortical visual impairment (CVI). How will the school know how she learns?
- I am a special education teacher and have a deaf-blind student in my class. At the last IEP meeting, I advised the team that she needs an interpreter. The supervisor refused to consider my request. Doesn't the law say that the district must provide an interpreter if the child needs this service?
- My child was born deaf. At the last meeting, we discussed his needs but did not develop an IEP. What services should the school provide?
- My daughter is in the deaf/hearing impaired program at school. She is active in sports. I enrolled her in a summer basketball camp sponsored by the school to improve her skills. The school refuses to provide interpreting services because the camp is not required. Is this right?
- My child has autism and is nonverbal. He gets angry and frustrated because he cannot communicate what he wants and needs. I want the school to teach him a way to communicate. The school claims that he cannot be taught. What can I do?
- My daughter has Rett Syndrome. She is high functioning but she cannot speak. I want her IEP to have communication goals. The school says she doesn't need communication goals because she can't speak.

8 Assistive Technology (A.T.)

- What is an assistive technology device?
- What are assistive technology services?
- My child has a severe hearing impairment. He needs an FM system. The school does not agree. What now?
- My child needs assistive technology. Can I request this evaluation?
- Some of my students with IEPs need assistive technology. When should the IEP team provide a technology device or service?
- The IEP team agreed that my child needs a laptop to do classwork. The school provides a laptop at school. He needs the laptop to do homework assignments. Can he bring the laptop home?
- Isn't assistive technology intended for students with severe physical disabilities?
- Some of my students with IEPs use calculators. They do not learn how to solve math problems because they depend on the calculator – isn't the calculator a crutch?
- My child has an A.T. device written into her IEP. The teacher doesn't know how to use the device so it isn't used. How can we make sure teachers are trained to use A.T. devices?
- What is Universal Design for Learning (UDL)?
- How can UDL help my child?

9 Transition to Life After School

- What are transition assessments?
- What are transition services?
- My 15 year-old needs help with transition planning. When will he be eligible for transition services?
- Is my child a member of the IEP team?
- My 15 year-old has cognitive impairments and cerebral palsy. He functions below his peer group. Does the IEP team have to develop measurable transition goals and plans, regardless of my child's skill levels?
- Can the IEP Team decide to address transition before age 16 (for example, at age 14)?
- My child is 14 years old. When I requested transition services and a transition plan, the IEP team said they don't have to provide transition services until he is 16. Is this correct?
- How does the IEP team determine measurable transition goals for my child?
- My tenth-grader has been in special ed since 3rd grade. He has learning disabilities. He is depressed and wants to drop out of school. I'm terrified about his future. Can transition planning help?
- At the last IEP meeting, the team decided that Vocational Rehabilitation would evaluate my child and provide transition services, including job training. Several months passed with no evaluation and no job training. The school says this is not their responsibility.
- What is "age of majority?"
- What happens in a transfer of rights?
- How will I know if or when educational rights transfer to my child?
- My son is nearly 18 so his educational rights will transfer soon. Without my input, I'm afraid he'll drop out or accept a diploma that will end his eligibility for special education and related services. What can I do to prevent this from happening?
- My child graduated from high school with a regular diploma. Is she still eligible for services from the public school?
- My 19 year-old earned a GED. Now he is having second thoughts. Is he still eligible for special education services?
- My child will soon graduate from high school. We received a document called "Summary of Academic Achievement and Functional Performance." What is this?
- My son just got a GED. Will he receive a Summary of Performance?
- Is the school required to provide documentation to determine a student's eligibility for Vocational Rehabilitation services?
- Is the school required to provide documentation that will allow my child to receive accommodations in college or another educational program?

10 Placement

- Who decides where my child will be placed?
- Do I have a say in decisions about my child's placement?
- How does the team decide on a child's placement?
- Are there any rules about placement decisions?

- What is the "continuum of alternative placements?"
- What is the relationship between placement decisions and supplementary aids, services, and supports?
- The IEP team talked about placing my daughter child in the "least restrictive environment." What does that mean?
- My 6th grader has learning disabilities. He has received special education services in a resource class for four years, but is still reading at the 2nd to 3rd grade level. I asked for one-on-one tutoring. The team said he must be educated in the regular classroom with special ed services from an aide. Is this correct?
- My child's school is an "inclusion school." What does that mean?
- My child is verbal and high functioning. The team placed her in a self-contained class of non-verbal boys with behavior problems. She needs to be in regular classes with other children her age. Any advice?
- Our son attends the regional school for children who are blind and have other visual impairments. He is doing well and meeting his IEP goals. The school sent a letter saying they have to place him in the "nearest school" to our home because of the "least restrictive environment" requirement. Does the "least restrictive environment" always mean the "nearest" school?
- The IEP team plans to change our child's placement over our objections. What can we do?
- The public school wants to place our child in a private school. If we agree, who is responsible for developing his IEP?
- Who is responsible for ensuring that an IEP is implemented in a private school?

11 Reviewing and Revising the IEP

- Who can request that an IEP be reviewed and revised?
- When can I request that my child's IEP be revised?
- I want to request a meeting to review and revise my child's IEP. Should I make my request in writing?
- What happens when the IEP team reviews and revises an IEP?
- My child isn't making progress so I asked for a meeting to revise the IEP. The school said they can't change the IEP because I signed it. Can a school refuse to review and revise an IEP for this reason?
- My child has had a "speech IEP" since first grade. Now he is in middle school. He is failing three classes. Is he entitled to special education services in these areas where he needs help?
- Our child takes a social skills class. He wants to take history and science as electives and we agree. The school says we must convene the IEP team to change these classes. Can't we do this without involving the entire IEP team?
- We revised our child's IEP by agreement. Because the IEP changed as a result of that meeting, the school says we are not entitled to the annual IEP review. Is this correct?
- If my child's IEP is reviewed and revised, does the entire IEP team have to attend the meeting?
- The school wants to amend my child's IEP without a meeting. We do not feel comfortable with this plan. Can we ask for a team meeting instead?

- Must our request to revise an IEP by agreement be in writing?
- We amended our child's IEP by agreement. We are worried that the teachers and service providers will not know about their new responsibilities. Will the school tell them about the changes in the IEP?
- I wrote a letter to request a meeting to review and revise my child's IEP a month ago. The school has not responded. How long does the school have to schedule a meeting?

12 Extended School Year Services

- Is ESY the same as summer school?
- Can the school charge a fee for ESY services?
- Are ESY services written into the IEP?
- My district provides ESY for a few weeks when summer school is in session. My child needs more than a few weeks of ESY, but the school says they don't have staff available.
- Should my child's placement for ESY services be in the least restrictive environment?
- The IEP team proposed that an aide provide my child's ESY program. Should a certified teacher provide these services?
- My child receives ESY services. Is the school responsible for transportation?
- Who decides if my child will receive Extended School Year services?
- My child has learning disabilities and has an IEP. He is in 6th grade but reads at the 3rd grade level. When I asked for ESY services, the team said he is not eligible because they only provide ESY for children with severe disabilities. Is this correct?
- When I requested ESY services, the team said my child would not benefit from the program they offer. Can they make decisions based on what they have available?
- What factors must the team consider in deciding if my child will receive ESY services?
- What is "regression and recoupment?"
- What role does "progress toward IEP goals and objectives" play in ESY decisions?
- My child zones out in class, so it's hard for him to learn and retain what he learns. Should he receive ESY services?
- Does my child have to demonstrate that she regressed before she can receive ESY services?
- When I requested ESY services for my child, the team said they use a "regression-recoupment" formula, and my daughter did not "regress enough" for ESY.
- How can I request ESY services for my child?

13 Transfers and Education Records

- We are moving to a new school district in the same state. Does the new school have to implement our child's current IEP?
- We moved to a new district in the same state. The school says they have to evaluate my child, determine if he is eligible, and develop a new IEP before they can provide any special education services. This will take months! Is this correct?
- We are moving to another state. Is the new school required to implement our child's current IEP?

- You say the receiving school must provide "comparable services" to students who transfer. What does "comparable services" mean?
- In a staff meeting our principal said, "We have a 90 day reprieve before we have to look at a transfer student's IEP." Is this right?
- A child with an IEP transferred into my class from another city in our state. How long does our district have to implement the IEP? How long before we are required to evaluate the student and write a new IEP?
- A child with autism transferred to our school. This child has a "Cadillac IEP" with one-to-one speech therapy and 40+ hours of ABA therapy a week. We are not prepared to provide these services. Can we require the child to stay home, without special education services, until our staff can develop a new IEP?
- A child received special education and related services under an IEP from a neighboring school district. That child moved to our district. What are our responsibilities?
- We plan to move this year. Our daughter will change schools. What steps can we take now to make the process go smoothly?
- We thought we had all of our child's education records. After the move, we discovered that we do not have some documents. Can the new school request the missing documents?
- A child transferred to our school from another state. The parent reports that their child has a disability and an IEP. The parent does not have any education records or a copy of the IEP. How can we provide comparable services if we don't have a copy of the IEP?

14 Resolving Parent-School Disputes

- I attended the first IEP meeting for my child. I don't agree with the school's proposed IEP. What should I do?
- My child's IEP states that the school will provide occupational therapy and physical therapy. I learned that the school did not provide any O.T. or P.T. services for several months. When I asked when they would make up the missed services, the team said they did not plan to provide any make-up services. What can I do?
- Are other options available to resolve disputes?
- What is mediation? How does it work?
- How much does mediation cost?
- If we resolve our dispute through mediation, what happens next?
- Do I have to request a due process hearing before mediation?
- What is a due process hearing? How does it work?
- My child is not making progress, so I asked for a meeting to review and revise the IEP. The team leader said I consented to the IEP so I have to wait until the next annual meeting before asking that it be changed. Is this true?
- My child is not making progress. How can I get the school to create an IEP with measurable goals?

- The goals in my child's IEP have not changed for years. How can I get the IEP team to write goals that are individualized to my child's needs?
- My child has autism. He needs to learn to communicate. The school provides two 30 -minute sessions of group speech therapy a week. This is not sufficient. I want additional services from a speech-language pathologist in the private sector. Can I request reimbursement?
- My 16 year-old has needs to learn basic living skills, problem solving, and survival skills before he leaves school. When I asked the IEP team to develop a transition plan that includes these skills, they said they focus on academic skills only. Is this correct?
- We had a comprehensive evaluation of our child by a psychologist in the private sector. We provided the evaluation to the IEP team. The team said they "considered" the evaluation but refused to use any information or recommendations from it. Can they do that?
- My child was born deaf. She has cochlear implants, so she can hear. The team wants to place her in a class with deaf children. The teacher uses American Sign Language. We want her to attend regular education classes with children her age so she learns to communicate by speaking. What can we do?
- What is Prior Written Notice?
- The IEP team decided to challenge my child by putting her in regular education classes, with accommodations. She is failing. How can I get her placement changed back into special ed?
- I agree with the services in the IEP but do not agree with the proposed placement. When I observed the placement, the teacher had too many students and was overwhelmed. The aide was out on maternity leave. The only opportunity the children had to interact with nondisabled children was at lunch. Even then, the children with disabilities sat at separate tables, not with other kids. How should I handle this?
- The IEP team presented an IEP that placed our child in a self-contained class. We did not agree. The speech therapist did not agree. Can the IEP team "vote" for a child's placement, over the objections of her parents and another team member?
- The IEP team wants to change our child's placement. We do not agree. What can we do?
- The IEP team wants to place my child in a special school across town. We want him to attend regular classes at our neighborhood school with his siblings. What can I do?
- Our child has processing problems and speech-language delays. She receives services from a speech-language therapist. Her regular education teacher is often impatient with her. How can we ensure that her teacher understands our child's disability and the impact it has on her ability to learn?

Introduction

- What is in This Book?
- Who Should Read This Book?
- How the Book is Organized
- How to Use the Book
- Are You Ready?

Do you have questions about IEPs? You aren't alone! Every week, the staff at Wrightslaw.com receive dozens of questions about IEPs.

Imagine these scenarios:

> "I don't agree that the proposed IEP is sufficient, but it is better than nothing. The IEP team says I have to 'take it or leave it!' Can't the school implement parts of the IEP while we continue to negotiate the issues where we don't agree?"

> "The school board attorney attended our last IEP meeting. The notice we received did not include the attorney on the list

of people who would attend. We felt blindsided. How should we handle this in the future?"

"My child has autism and is nonverbal. He gets angry and frustrated because he cannot communicate what he wants and needs. I want the school to teach him a way to communicate. The school claims that he cannot be taught. What can I do?"

"My 16 year-old needs to learn daily living skills, problem solving, and survival skills before he leaves school. When I asked the IEP team to develop a transition plan that includes these skills, they said they focus on academic skills only."

"We had a comprehensive evaluation of our child by a psychologist in the private sector. We provided the evaluation to our child's IEP team. The team said they 'considered' the evaluation but refused to use any information or recommendations from it."

What would you say? What would you do? What are your child's rights? Do you have rights?

What Is in This Book?

In ***Wrightslaw: All About IEPs,*** we answer more than 200 questions and guide you through dozens of scenarios. We introduce key legal issues that you are likely to encounter if you have a child with a disability who receives special education services. We outline your rights and responsibilities, and explain the law in plain language you can understand.

We introduce some legal terms because parents, teachers, service providers, and advocates need to be familiar with these terms. We want to demystify the law so it is less intimidating.

As you read the answers to these questions and scenarios, you will learn that the law varies from state to state. You may find answers to your questions in your state special education regulations. You may need to contact the Parent Training & Information Center (PTI) or Disability Rights organization in your state. You may need to consult with an attorney who has expertise in special education law and litigation.

Although you will receive guidance from ***Wrightslaw: All About IEPs***, this book is not a substitute for professional legal advice. We suggest strategies to resolve problems. We do not advise you to pursue litigation without assistance from an attorney.

We urge you to find creative ways to resolve parent-school disputes without litigation. Litigation is expensive, time-consuming, stressful, and should be reserved for serious disputes that cannot be resolved in other ways. We advise you to deal with conflict directly and try to negotiate an acceptable solution.

Wrightslaw: All About IEPs includes scenarios and questions, including these:

- Is the IEP team required to consider information and input provided by parents? (Chapter 2 – Your Child's IEP Team and IEP Meetings)

- As a parent, do I have to give my consent before the school can implement the IEP? (Chapter 3 – Parental Participation and Consent)
- What are measurable IEP goals? (Chapter 4 – Present Levels, Measurable IEP Goals, Special Education Services)
- Are there limits on the speech, physical, and occupational therapy a child can receive? (Chapter 5 – Related Services, Supplementary Aids and Services)
- What is the difference between accommodations and modifications? (Chapter 6 - Progress, Accommodations and Modifications, Alternate Assessments)
- When should the IEP team refer a child for a functional behavioral assessment? (Chapter 7 – Special Factors in the IEP)
- Some of my students with IEPs need assistive technology. When should the IEP team provide a technology device or service? (Chapter 8 – Assistive Technology)
- My child is 14. When I requested transition services and a transition plan, the IEP team said they don't have to provide transition services until he is 16. Is this correct? (Chapter 9 - Transition)
- The IEP team plans to change our child's placement over our objections. What can we do? (Chapter 10 – Placement)
- If my child's IEP is reviewed and revised, does the entire IEP team have to attend the meeting? (Chapter 11 – Review and Revising IEPs)
- What factors must the team consider in deciding if my child will receive ESY services? (Chapter 12 – ESY Services)
- In a staff meeting our principal said, "We have a 90 day reprieve before we have to look at a transfer student's IEP." Is this right? (Chapter 13 – Transfers and Education Records)
- I attended the first IEP meeting for my child. I don't agree with the school's proposed IEP. What should I do? (Chapter 14 – Resolving Parent-School Disputes)

Wrightslaw: All About IEPs is not an encyclopedia of every question a parent, teacher or advocate could ask. The book is not a manual about how to write SMART IEPs.

Who Should Read This Book?

If you are the parent of a child with a disability, you represent your child's interests. To effectively advocate for your child, you need to know your child's rights, and your rights and responsibilities. When you negotiate for special education services, you have two goals: to get quality services and to maintain healthy working relationships with school personnel.

If you are a teacher, related service provider, or school administrator, you may receive confusing, conflicting information about IEPs. You need reliable information about the legal requirements for IEPs.

If you teach special education, school psychology, school administration, or education law courses, your students need to learn how to find answers to their questions about what the law requires of them.

If you are an attorney or advocate who represents children with disabilities, you need to have ***Wrightslaw: All About IEPs*** on your desk and in your briefcase.

How This Book is Organized

The questions and scenarios in this book are organized by topic into fourteen chapters. The book includes a table of questions, two appendices, a glossary of terms, a bibliography of references, and an index.

How to Use This Book

As you read these questions and answers, you may feel like you are having a conversation with Pete, Pam and Sue. Or you may feel like you are reading an advice column. When you read a question that captures your interest, you wonder what advice we will give.

You will find endnotes at the end of each chapter. These endnotes are the authority we relied upon in the answers. If you take this book to school meetings (and we hope you will), you will know the law, regulation, commentary, or government publication that supports each answer.

Appendix A includes the law about IEPs from the Individuals with Disabilities Education Act. Appendix B includes the federal regulations about IEPs.

If you go to an IEP meeting and are told, "We don't do things that way in this district," you will know that the federal law and regulations are the minimum standards that all schools must comply with. Compliance with the law is not optional.

Learn more about the law, regulations, commentary, legal citations, and other legal references at:

www.wrightslaw.com/bks/aaiep/resources.htm

Wrightslaw: All About IEPs includes advocate's tips, checklists, and recommended resources.

Are You Ready?

You can't loiter in the introduction forever. It's time to learn about IEPs. Grab a highlighter or a pen.

If you are ready to learn, turn this page.

1 Getting Started

- Effective Advocacy
- 4 Mistakes Parents Make
- Planning and Preparing
- Advocacy Tools
- 5 Rules for Successful IEP Meetings

In this chapter, you will learn how to be an effective advocate for your child. You will learn that the keys to successful IEP meetings are preparing, organizing information, and knowing how to present requests.

You will learn to use the IEP Meeting Worksheet to prepare and the Parent Agenda to express concerns and make requests.

You will learn "4 Mistakes Parents Make" and how to avoid them. You will also learn the "5 Rules of Successful IEP Meetings."

Effective Advocacy

Who is your child's first teacher? You are. Who is your child's most important role model? You are. Who is responsible for your child's welfare? You are. Who has your child's best interests at heart? You do.

When you attend IEP meetings, you represent your child's interests. Your goals are to negotiate with the school, obtain quality special education services for your child, and build healthy working relationships with school personnel.

4 Mistakes Parents Make

1. Failing to make a long term plan for their child's education or the future

Some parents do not think about the future until it arrives. They don't have long-range goals for their child. They don't think about what they want their child to be able to do when he leaves the public school system. They don't have a plan.

Imagine your child as a young adult. What should your child be able to do? Do you envision your child working at a job and raising a family? Will he be a member of the community? What does he need to learn so he is prepared for "further education, employment, and independent living?"[1]

Your child's special education is a long-term project. A plan will help you stay focused, anticipate problems, and prepare for the future. Your plan should include academic and behavioral, social, and emotional goals, including hobbies, personal interests, sports and fitness, family, friendships, and the community. Your plan should be revisited and revised as your child grows.

2. Not understanding their child's disability and allowing the school to make decisions about their child's special education

Some parents don't understand their child's disability, how the disability affects the child's learning, or how the child needs to be taught.

They don't know what services and supports their child needs. They don't know if their child is making progress. They don't know the steps they must take to ensure that their child receives an appropriate education.

These parents have given decision-making authority to the school. They assume school personnel will make wise decisions about educating their child. The school may have low expectations for the child and parents tend to accept the school's low expectations.

If you do not ensure that your child receives an appropriate education and learns the skills necessary to be an independent, self-sufficient member of the community, you will deal with the outcome long past childhood.

And if you are tempted to lower your expectations, consider this: Your child will internalize your low expectations. A vicious cycle begins. Low expectations lead to low achievement.

3. Forgetting to keep your emotions under control

As a parent, your emotions may be your Achilles' heel.

If you are like many parents, when you learn that your child has a disability, you turn to school personnel and medical specialists for help. If you and the school disagree about what is appropriate for your child, you may feel shocked and angry. You may feel betrayed by the system you trusted. Once lost, trust is hard to regain.

4. Not documenting events and conversations in writing

"I told the IEP team that my child was not making progress. The team agreed and said they would provide more services."

> *"If it was not written down, it was not said. If it was not written down, it did not happen."*
> -Pete Wright

Assume the school did not provide more services. How can you prove they agreed to do so?

One common mistake parents make is not writing things down as they happen. When you write things down — in a letter, log, or journal — you are taking steps to protect your child's interests.

In general, the best way to document events and problems is by writing short polite letters to the school. Describe what happened or what you were told. Use facts, not emotions. Your letters will become part of your child's file.

Be sure to keep a copy of all correspondence for your records.

Planning and Preparing

Effective advocacy comes from research, planning, and preparation. When you know a meeting is scheduled, it is time to prepare.

Gather information and review your child's file. Review the current IEP. Use test scores to monitor progress. Identify problems and propose solutions.

Gather Information and Review the File

Make an appointment to talk with your child's teachers and/or therapists.

Do the teachers and related services providers think he is making satisfactory progress? What areas are they concerned about?

Take notes. Ask questions if you do not understand.

Make an appointment to observe your child in class.

Talk with your child about school. What is he learning? Does he believe he is making good progress?

File all loose documents in your child's file. Make sure you have all recent test data.

Review the Current IEP

If your child has an IEP, review the goals. Did your child master the goals? Was mastery complete or partial? How do you know? Do you have objective data that supports your beliefs?

Review the periodic reports of your child's progress toward the IEP goals. Do the progress reports indicate that your child is on track to master the goals? If he was not making sufficient progress, did the IEP team meet to review and revise the IEP? What steps did the team make to help him meet the goals?

Use Test Scores to Monitor Progress

Review the test results, including state and district testing. Do you know what the tests measure? How did your child do?

Compare your child's current test data to earlier test data. Is your child making progress? How much progress? Do you have concerns about your child's program or progress?

Identify Problems and Propose Solutions

Review your notes from prior meetings. Review your contact log. Any unresolved issues? Any problems you want to bring up at the next meeting?

When you review your child's file, the current IEP, new test scores, and your notes, you will think about issues you want the team to address. List these issues, your questions, concerns, and proposed solutions.

If you know the perceptions of your school district, it will be easier to devise win-win solutions to problems. Answer these questions.

- How do you view your child's problems?
- How does the school view your child's problems?
- How is the school likely to respond to your concerns?
- How will you handle the school's response?
- What solutions will you propose?

Advocacy Tools

Use the Pre-Meeting Worksheet

Use the Pre-Meeting Worksheet to prepare for the meeting. Fill in the information about the meeting time and date, location, purpose of the meeting, and who requested the meeting. As you continue to prepare, you will be able to answer more of the questions.

At the top of the Worksheet, write "Who, What, Why, When, Where, How, Explain." (5 Ws + H + E) If you write this down, you are more likely to ask questions.

Answer these questions in your Worksheet:

- What do you want?
- What does the school want?
- What action do you want the school to take?
- How motivated are they to give you what you want?

Pre-Meeting Worksheet

Location: ______________________________

Date: ______________________________

What is the purpose of the meeting? ______________________________

Who requested the meeting? ______________________________

Who will attend the meeting (e.g., teachers, administrators, parent, child)? ______________

What do you want? ______________________________

What do they want? ______________________________

What action do you want them to take? ______________________________

How motivated are they to give you what you want? ______________________________

What will prevent them from giving you what you want? ______________________________

How can you alleviate their concerns? ______________________________

Learn more about "Preparing for Meetings" in Chapter 25, ***Wrightslaw: From Emotions to Advocacy, 2nd Edition.***

- What will prevent them from giving you what you want?
- How can you address their concerns and fears?

Prepare a Parent Agenda

You can use a parent agenda to:

- Prepare for meetings
- Identify concerns and list problems
- Make requests and propose solutions to problems
- Identify issues and problems that are not resolved
- Improve parent-school relationships

If you use a parent agenda, send your agenda to the IEP team members before the meeting. Assume that some of the people will not read your agenda until they are in the meeting. Bring extra copies for people who misplaced or lost their copies.

Practice Making Requests

When you make requests, practice. When you practice, you prepare. Practice causes your anxiety to drop. State your problems or concerns clearly and concisely. Offer suggestions about how you want the problem to be resolved. Be open to options suggested by the school.

Your Image

When you dress neatly and conservatively for school meetings, you convey a professional image. When you organize your child's file and bring the file to IEP meetings, you send the message that you expect to develop a professional partnership with other team members.

When you arrive early for an IEP meeting, you have time to relax and focus on what you want to accomplish.

Your interpersonal style affects how you feel and behave at IEP meetings. If you are a controller, you are likely to feel out of control at IEP meetings. If you are eager to please, your desire to be liked may cause you to agree to anything the school proposes. If you are a conflict-avoider, you may keep your concerns about your child's education to yourself. Look in the mirror. Do you need to change your style?

5 Rules of Successful IEP Meetings

Here are five rules for successful IEP meetings. Keep these rules in mind as you prepare for the next IEP meeting.

1. Know what you want

Make requests in writing. If you make a verbal request, be sure to follow up with a letter. If you have a problem, think about possible solutions to the problem. Describe the problem and solutions in clear language. You want the IEP team members to understand the problem and your proposed solutions.

When you are prepared, you can participate effectively in meetings. Answer these questions:

- What do you want?

IEP Meeting Worksheet

Child's Name:

Date:

School:

Child's Need/ Parent Request	School's Response	Resolved	Start Date	Responsible Person

Learn more about "Meeting Strategies" in Chapter 26, *Wrightslaw: From Emotions to Advocacy, 2nd Edition.*

- What action do you want the IEP team to take?
- What facts support your request?

If the team ignores or belittles your solutions, it is important to document this in a polite follow-up letter after the meeting.

2. Do not blame or criticize

When you describe problems or express concerns to an IEP team, stick to the facts. Do not blame or criticize. If a team member reacts defensively, be careful!

When people feel defensive, anxious, or angry, their ability and willingness to solve problems drops. If you stick to the facts, you make it more likely that the team will develop creative solutions to problems, rather than feel defensive.

3. Protect the parent-school relationship

In parent-school negotiations, you need to separate your personal relationships from the problems. If you view a person across the table as the problem, you are likely to feel mistrustful and angry.

When you negotiate, you have two interests:

- To solve problems
- To protect parent-school relationships

You will negotiate again!

4. Seek win-win solutions to problems

When IEP teams develop mutually acceptable solutions to problems, team members are committed to the success of their solutions. If negotiations shift to a win-lose perspective, and one side loses, expect them to sabotage the solution.

5. Understand the school's position

To be a successful negotiator, you must be able to step into the shoes of the people on the other side of the table. You need to be able to answer these questions:

- What are their perceptions? How do the school members of the IEP team see the problem?
- What are their interests? What do they want?
- What are their fears? What are they afraid will happen if they give you what you want?

When you can answer these questions, it will be easier to develop solutions that allow you and the school to meet your child's needs.

In Summation

In this chapter, you learned that you represent your child's interests as you negotiate with the IEP team for special education services.

You learned about four common mistakes parents make and how to avoid them. You learned the steps to prepare for IEP meetings. You have a step-by-step plan to prepare for meetings.

You know how to use the Pre-Meeting Worksheet to prepare for meetings and the Parent Agenda to make requests.

Let's move on to the next chapter and learn about IEP teams and IEP meetings.

Endnote

1. 20 U.S.C. § 1400(d)

2 IEP Teams and IEP Meetings

- Members of Your Child's IEP Team
- People with Special Knowledge and Expertise
- Excusing Members from IEP Meetings
- New Ways to Participate in IEP Meetings
- Attorneys at IEP Meetings
- Handling "Draft IEPs" and "Pre-IEP Meetings"
- Recording Meetings

In this chapter, you will find answers to your questions about IEP teams and IEP team meetings. You will learn about required IEP team members and how to include others who have special knowledge and expertise on the IEP team.

You will learn who may be excused from an IEP meeting and what steps must be taken before a member can be excused.

You will also get answers to questions about draft IEPs, pre-IEP meetings, and recording meetings. You will learn why the law discourages attorneys at IEP meetings.

Members of Your Child's IEP Team

During an IEP meeting, our special ed director said, "Parents are not members of the child's IEP team." We were astounded! Is this true?

No! Parents have always been members of their child's IEP team. The required members of your child's IEP team include:[1]

- The child's parents
- At least one of your child's regular education teachers
- At least one of your child's special education teachers or service providers
- A school district representative who is qualified to provide or supervise the special education instruction, is knowledgeable about the general education curriculum and is knowledgeable about district resources
- An individual who can interpret the instructional implications of evaluation results
- Others who have knowledge or expertise about your child
- The child, if appropriate (If the team will consider your child's transition needs, the team must invite your child to the meeting.)

Which teachers should be members of my child's IEP team?

Your child's team must include at least one of your child's special education teachers or related service providers and at least one of your child's regular education teachers.[2]

My child is in regular education classes and has several teachers. Which regular education teacher should be on the IEP team?

The regular education teacher on your child's team should be one who is (or who may be) responsible for implementing part of the IEP.

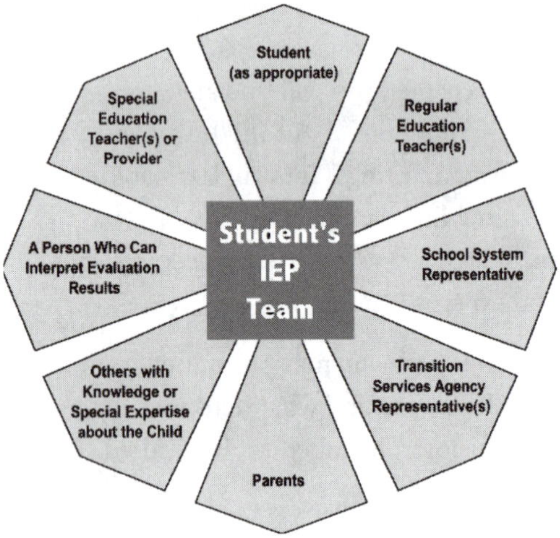

If more than one regular education teacher will implement part of the IEP, the district may designate which teacher or teachers will serve on the IEP team.[3]

What is the regular education teacher's role at the IEP meeting?

The regular education teacher knows the curriculum and what students are expected to learn and do. This teacher should participate in decisions about how to teach your child.

With input from the regular education teacher, the team can determine what accommodations, supplementary aids and services, and modifications your child needs to learn and make progress. She can also initiate discussion of appropriate behavioral interventions, supports, and strategies.[4]

If all regular education teachers don't attend the IEP meeting, how can they provide input into my child's IEP? How will these teachers know what's in the IEP?

The IEP team needs to seek input from all teachers who do not attend the IEP meeting.[5]

Your school district must ensure that all teachers and service providers have access to your child's IEP. They must be informed about the accommodations, modifications, and supports they are required to provide in accordance with your child's IEP.[6]

My child has behavior problems that prevent him from learning in the classroom. Can the IEP team help?

Yes. Your child's behavior is having a negative impact on his learning and the learning of other children. Your child's regular education teacher should be trained in positive behavior interventions and strategies. The district must ensure that the regular education teacher participates and provides input during the IEP meeting.[7]

For more information about services to children with behavior problems, see Chapter 7, Special Factors in the IEP.

If the principal is a certified teacher, can he fill the role of the regular education teacher on my child's IEP team?

Probably not. If the principal is a certified teacher, he/she does not qualify as the regular education teacher on the team unless he actually implements the IEP as your child's classroom teacher.

In some cases, an IEP team member may fill more than one role.

Who is the district representative? What is this person's role?

The school district representative is an individual who is knowledgeable about the general education curriculum and resources available in the district. The district representative must be qualified to provide special education services or supervise special education teachers.

In many cases, the school district representative is the special education director, supervisor, or school principal.[8]

Is my child a member of the IEP team?

Yes! Your child is a member and should attend IEP meetings when you decide this is appropriate. In deciding if your child will attend an IEP meeting, you need to answer two questions:

- Will your child benefit from attending the IEP meeting?
- Will your child's input help the team develop an appropriate IEP?

Attending IEP meetings is a great way for children and adolescents to learn self-advocacy skills.

When children attend their IEP meetings, they learn about problems related to their disabilities and strategies to deal with these problems.

My son will be 16 soon. Should he attend the next IEP meeting?

Yes, your son should attend the next IEP meeting. He needs to have input into decisions that will affect him.

Since he is nearly 16, the IEP team should be preparing for transition. Transition services must be included in the IEP that is in effect when he turns 16 as explained in Chapter 9. The school must invite you and your son to transition IEP meetings.

Should the IEP team include a person who is qualified to conduct specific diagnostic assessments?

No, the IEP team is not required to include a person who is qualified to conduct a particular diagnostic assessment.[9] The IEP team must include a person who is able to interpret the instructional and educational implications of tests and evaluations.[10]

Is the IEP team required to consider information and input provided by parents?

Yes. As the parent member of your child's IEP team, you are an equal participant in meetings.

You provide essential information about your child's strengths, weaknesses, and needs. You also share concerns about your child's special education program.

You represent your child's interests. The IEP team will make decisions about your child's needs for special education services, related services, and supplementary aids and services. The team decides how your child will be involved in and make progress in the regular education curriculum and how your child will participate in state and district assessments.

People with Special Knowledge and Expertise

As a parent, can I invite other people to the IEP meeting?

Yes. You and the school can invite people who have special knowledge and expertise about your child to IEP meetings.
Think about a person who knows your child well–for example, a friend, family

member, minister, priest, or rabbi.

Your child's grandparents may have a special relationship with your child. Many grandparents want to help their grandchild and are eager to attend IEP meetings.[11]

Do not go to IEP meetings alone. Many parents describe IEP meetings as intimidating and overwhelming. Both parents need to make every effort to attend. If this is impossible, bring a friend who can act as a note-taker and provide support. Having a note-taker or support person helps you pay attention to what happens, without worrying that you will miss important information.

> *"I want the aide who works with our child to attend the IEP meeting. The principal said, 'No! If I do this for you, I have to do it for all parents.' I showed the principal the statement in IDEA that parents can invite people who have knowledge or expertise about the child to IEP meetings."*
>
> 34 CFR § 300.321 (a)(6) &(c)

Must the person I ask to attend the IEP meeting be an advocate or evaluator?

No. The law allows you to invite individuals who have knowledge or special expertise about your child.[12] You decide who meets these criteria. There is no requirement that you may only invite professionals.

You may also invite your child's related services providers if they are not members of the team.[13] Independent educational professionals, including consultants, advocates, and tutors, who are familiar with your child, can be particularly helpful.

Should I let the school know who I plan to bring ahead of time?

Yes. No one likes surprises. The school must notify you about the purpose, time and location of the meeting, and who will attend. The school must also advise you of your right and their right to invite other people who have knowledge or special expertise about your child.

These requirements help you know what to expect. If you plan to bring other individuals to the meeting, you need to inform the school ahead of time.

Our school designated one speech therapist to attend IEP meetings for all students who receive speech therapy. My child's speech therapist does not attend. Shouldn't the speech therapist who works with my child attend the IEP meetings?

Yes. Your child's speech language therapist should attend her IEP meetings. If your child's speech language therapy will be discussed in the meeting, the person who provides this therapy should attend.

A speech language therapist who does not work with your child does not have the necessary knowledge about your child.

The decision to appoint one therapist to attend IEP meetings for all children who receive speech therapy is convenient for the school. This practice is not appropriate and does not comply with the legal requirements for IEP team members.[14]

I am the sign language interpreter for a deaf child who attends regular education classes. I work closely with her and make educational decisions on her behalf. I want to participate in her IEP meetings. My supervisor says my input is unnecessary.

Interpreting is a related service.[15] Related services personnel should be included on the child's team when a particular related service will be discussed, at the request of the child's parents or the school.

For example, if the child's evaluation indicates the child needs a specific related service, the school should ensure that a qualified provider of that service either (1) attends the IEP meeting, or (2) provides a written recommendation concerning the nature, frequency, and amount of service to be provided to the child. This written recommendation may be a part of the evaluation report.[16]

The parent and the school may invite people who have special knowledge and expertise to IEP meetings. As the interpreter, you have special knowledge and expertise. One solution may be for the parents to invite you to attend her IEP meetings.

Excusing Members from IEP Meetings

If a member of the IEP team wants to be excused, do I have to agree?

No. If you do not agree, the member may not be excused. The law includes two circumstances that allow a team member to be excused from a meeting. If their area of the curriculum or related service will not be discussed or modified during the meeting, they may be excused. If their area will be discussed or modified, the individual must submit a written report to the parent and school team members before the meeting. In both circumstances, you must agree to excuse the team member and you must give your consent **in writing.**[17]

The problem with this provision is that you may not know what areas of the curriculum and related services will be discussed. Assume an absent member submits a written report. The team members, including you, cannot question the report. To answer questions that arise during the meeting, the school will have to schedule another meeting.

Do things right the first time. For the initial or annual IEP meeting, all team members should participate. If a meeting is to review or revise a specific or limited issue, then fewer members may result in a more efficient meeting.

If the team asks you to consent for a member to be excused and you do not agree, write a short polite letter to the team. Explain that you do not consent to excusing this member because the individual has valuable information and insights to share with the group.

At the last IEP meeting, some members did not show up. What can I do to prevent this from happening again?

Write a letter that describes what happened. In general, send the letter to the IEP team leader or supervisor who has the power to resolve the problem.

In your letter, explain that you received a notice that included the names of team members who would attend the IEP meeting. You were surprised and disappointed when these members did not attend. Because these members were absent, the team did not have information or advice from these members.

You thought that if a team member's area would be discussed, that person was required to attend or to submit a written report to the team and the parent ahead of time. Before a team member can be excused, the school must agree and the parent must give written consent. Is your understanding correct?

If you think a team member's absence prevented the team from developing an IEP that meets your child's needs, request another team meeting. Ask that all IEP team members attend.[18]

At our last IEP team meeting, several people left before they read their reports or gave input. I thought IEP team members were supposed to provide information and answer questions. Am I wrong?

You are right. The purpose of the IEP meeting is to discuss your child's needs and develop an IEP with goals to meet those needs. All team members are expected to participate in discussions and decisions. If a member needs to be excused, the team should reschedule the meeting until all members can participate in the IEP decision-making process.[19]

Are there penalties for schools that routinely excuse IEP team members?

Yes. All districts are subject to the state's monitoring and enforcement provisions.[20] A school district that routinely excuses IEP team members from meetings is not in compliance with the law.

Can a parent demand that a member of the IEP team be excluded from a meeting?

No. A parent does not have a right to exclude a team member from an IEP meeting.[21]

You should not make demands. If you make demands, you set the stage for a battle you cannot win. Other members of the team will have less respect for you and your concerns.

When you request services for your child, you need to keep relations businesslike and unemotional. This may require a large helping of self-discipline.

One of your goals is to share your concerns and persuade the team to act on these concerns. If you demand, you will not accomplish this goal.

If you have trouble controlling your emotions, consider getting help from an educational advocate or advice from an attorney who specializes in this area of law.

How often are IEP meetings held?

IEP meetings must be held at least annually, and more often when necessary.[22] Meetings should be held more often if a child is not making expected progress and a parent or teacher requests a meeting to review or revise the IEP.

To learn about reviewing and revising IEPs, please read Chapter 11.

New Ways to Participate in IEP Meetings

Private speech and occupational therapists work with our child and provide goals for her IEP. The school advised us that their goals cannot be included unless they attend the IEP meeting. The therapists are 125 miles away. Can they participate in the meeting but not attend in person?

Yes. People with special expertise about your child can be team members without attending a meeting in person. The law provides alternative ways to participate in meetings. You and your school district can agree to use alternative means to participate in meetings, including video conferences and conference calls.[23]

Attorneys at IEP Meetings

May the school district bring their attorney to an IEP meeting? May we bring an attorney?

Yes, the parent and the school district may bring attorneys to meetings. Except for the Resolution Session, no statute or regulation prohibits this practice.[24]

However, in most cases, we do not recommend it.

When attorneys attend IEP meetings, their presence often creates an adversarial atmosphere. IEP team members are those who have an interest in or knowledge about the child.[25] The parents and school may invite individuals who have knowledge or special expertise about the child. In most cases, an attorney will not meet these requirements.

The school board attorney attended our last IEP meeting. The notice we received did not include the attorney on the list of people who would attend. We felt blindsided. How should we handle this in the future?

Write a polite, businesslike letter to the IEP team leader or supervisor who has the power to resolve the problem. Describe what happened and your reaction. Include information from other questions in this chapter about who may be invited to a child's IEP meeting and the requirement for notifying parents in advance of who will attend.

Handling Draft IEPs and Pre-IEP Meetings

At the last IEP meeting, I was presented with a "draft IEP." I felt that the school made decisions about my child's special education program without input from me. Is this legal?

The answer depends on several issues. Schools are not permitted to complete a final IEP before the IEP meeting. If the team develops draft proposals before the meeting, they "should provide the parents with a copy of its draft proposals."

You need time to review the school's proposals before the meeting so you can discuss them.

The commentary to the federal regulations discourages schools from preparing draft IEPs because the drafts may inhibit full and open discussion of the child's needs. [26]

School staff may prepare to discuss your child's evaluation results and their preliminary recommendations. At the beginning of the meeting, they must clairfy that any services in the draft are recommendations for discussion.

As the parent who represents your child's interests, you need to bring your questions, concerns, and recommendations to the IEP meeting. In your role as an active participant, you need to ensure that the services the school agrees to provide are described fully and written clearly in the final IEP document. See Chapter 4 about Developing the IEP.

Is it legal for the school to have "pre-IEP meetings" that exclude the child's parents?

The law does not mention pre-IEP meetings. When parents arrive at the school and realize that school personnel held an IEP meeting without them, they know the school staff made decisions about what the school will and will not offer.

Although these meetings are convenient for school personnel, the practice of excluding parents leads to mistrust. Pre-IEP meetings violate the spirit of the law. These meetings cause mistrust and conflict. They destroy the trust that is essential in healthy parent-school relationships.

Recording Meetings

During IEP meetings, so many people talk at the same time, I can't keep track. When I get home, I can't remember what we agreed to. Can I make a recording of my child's IEP meetings so I can review them later?

Maybe. Federal law does not prohibit a parent or school official from recording IEP meetings. State departments of education or school districts can require, prohibit, limit, or regulate the use of recording devices at IEP meetings.[27]

Request a copy of the written policy so you know the limitations.

There should be no conversation at an IEP meeting that cannot be repeated or taped. If your school has a policy that prohibits parents from recording meetings, that policy must include exceptions.

A court has held that a parent had a right to record her child's IEP meetings.[28]

As a courtesy, advise the school ahead of time of your intent to record the meeting.

Advocate's TIP

We put a recorder on the table, turn it on, and identify the time, date, place, and purpose of the meeting. If a school employee tells us to turn the recorder off, we pick up the microphone. We politely ask the person to speak into the microphone, to state their name and that the school refuses to allow the parent to make an audio record of the child's school meeting. In most cases, the person who objected says, " I guess it's ok."

by Brice Palmer, Vermont Advocate

In Summation

In this chapter, you learned about IEP teams and IEP team meetings. You learned how to include people with special knowledge on the IEP team. You learned the steps the school must take before excusing an IEP team member.

You also learned about draft IEPs, pre-IEP meetings, and recording meetings.

In the next chapter, you will learn about your parental role, consent, and when you need to give consent. You will find out why it is essential that you be an active participant in developing your child's IEP.

Endnotes

1. 20 U.S.C. § 1414(d)(1)(B); 34 C.F.R. § 300.321
2. 20 U.S.C. § 1414(d)(1)(B)(ii)&(iii); 34 C.F.R. § 300.321(a)(2)&(3)
3. Commentary in 71 FR at 46675
4. 34 C.F.R. § 300.324(a)(3)
5. Appendix A, Question #26; Commentary in 64 FR (1999) at 12478; www.ed.gov/policy/speced/leg/idea/brief3.html
6. 34 C.F.R. § 300.323(d)
7. 34 C.F.R. § 300.324(a)(3)(i)
8. 34 C.F.R. § 300.321(a)(4)(ii)&(iii)
9. Commentary in 71 FR at 46670
10. 20 U.S.C. § 1414(d)(1)(B)(v); 34 C.F.R. § 300.321(a)(5)
11. 34 C.F.R. § 300.321(c)
12. 34 C.F.R. § 300.321(c)
13. Commentary in 71 FR at 46669-70
14. Commentary in 71 FR at 46675
15. 20 U.S.C. § 1401(20)(A); 34 C.F.R. §300.34(c)(4)
16. Committee Reports on the IDEA Amendments of 1997, H. Rep. No. 105-95, p. 103; S. Rep. No. 105-17, p. 23)
17. 34 C.F.R. § 300.321 (e)(2)
18. Commentary in 71 FR at 46676
19. Commentary in 71 FR at 46674-76
20. Commentary in 71 FR at 46674
21. Commentary in 71 FR at 46673
22. 34 C.F.R. § 300.324 (b)(1)(i)

23. 20 U.S.C. § 1414(f); 34 C.F.R. § 300.328

24. 20 U.S.C. § 1415(f)(1)(B)(1)(III)

25. www.nde.state.ne.us/SPED/iepproj/prepare/team.html

26. Commentary in 71 FR at 46678

27. Appendix A, Question #21, OSEP Memo www.ed.gov/policy/speced/guid/idea/letters/2003-2/redact060403iep2q2003.pdf

28. Letter and Memo from OSEP

www.ed.gov/policy/speced/guid/idea/letters/2003-2/redact060403iep2q2003.pdf; *V.W. and R.W. v. Favolise and Colchester Board of Education*, 131 F.R.D. 654 (D. Conn. 1990)

3 Parental Participation and Consent

- Your Parental Role
- Parental Consent
- Parent Participation

If you are like most parents, you may feel confused, frustrated, and intimidated at school meetings. How can you get the school to respond to your requests? How can you get the school to provide the services and support your child needs? What is your role?

The law is clear. Parents have the right to participate in the meeting when their child's IEP is developed.

In this chapter, you will learn about your parental role, consent, and when you must give consent. You will learn why you need to be an active participant in developing your child's IEPs.

Your Parental Role

The law gives you the power to make educational decisions for your child. Do not be afraid to use your power. Use it wisely. A good education is the most important gift you can give your child.

As your child's parent, you are a key member of the IEP team. You are not a spectator. You are an active participant.

What is my role at my child's IEP meeting?

As the parent of a child with special educational needs, you represent your child's interests. You are an essential part of the IEP process. When you negotiate with the school on your child's behalf, you increase the odds that your child will receive a quality educational program. Ask questions and make suggestions during team meetings.

How to Ask Questions

Do not feel intimidated when asking questions. The people running schools have an obligation to explain to parents what they do. People who run schools sometimes fend off questions with assertions that they know best because of their experience and expertise or because "research" says so.

Real experts don't hide behind their expertise. They explain what they do, cite specific research with clear explanations about why this research is reliable and relevant.

Homeroom by Karin Chenoweth at www.washingtonpost.com/wp-dyn/articles/33056-2004Aug25.html

What should I expect in an IEP meeting?

The IEP is designed to be a collaborative meeting. Members of the IEP team represent the diverse aspects and needs of the child. Nevertheless, while it should be a team effort, you may have to negotiate instead of collaborate, so be prepared to do both.

During each IEP meeting, you and other team members will discuss:

- Your child's present levels of academic achievement and functional performance
- Measurable IEP goals designed to meet your child's unique needs
- Special education services, related services, and supplementary aids and services the school will provide
- How your child's progress will be measured and how you will be advised of progress
- Your child's placement (where your child will receive services)

Begin to prepare for the IEP meeting by answering these questions:

- What are your child's strengths and weaknesses?
- How does your child's disability affect his or her ability to learn?
- What goals do you have for this year? What do you want your child to learn and be able to do after a year of special education?

- Do you have concerns about your child's special education program? Make a list of your concerns and proposed solutions.
- Is your child making progress? Is your child regressing? How do you know?
- What are your long-term goals for your child?

Chapter 1 describes what you need to know before you go to an IEP meeting. You will find many ideas and tips about how to prepare for IEP meetings throughout this book.

Parental Consent

What is "consent?"

The school must obtain your consent before your child is evaluated, reevaluated, or placed in special education. Consent means more than giving your permission to proceed. It also means:

- You have been fully informed in your native language of all information relevant to the activity for which the school needs your consent.
- You understand and "agree in writing"[1] that the school may carry out the activity for which they need your consent.
- You understand that granting your consent is voluntary.
- You may revoke your consent at any time.[2]

As a parent, do I have to give my consent before the school can implement the IEP?

Yes. The special education law and regulations require parents to give informed consent before the school can provide services in the initial IEP.[3] Consent for subsequent IEPs varies from state to state.

Some states require written consent to implement IEPs on a year-to-year basis. Check your state special education regulations to learn what your state requires.

Your State Special Education Regulations

You'll find your state special education regulations on the website for your state Department of Education. Go to the Wrightslaw Yellow Pages for Kids, Directory of State Departments of Education at www.yellowpagesforkids.com/help/seas.htm.

Find your state and click on the state DOE website link. Search this state site for "special education regulations." You will also find a contact number if you want to call to request a print copy.

My child has received special education services for years. I have never been asked to sign an IEP. Does the law require my signature?

Many parents have questions about signing their child's IEP. For the initial

IEP, the law requires the school to get your written consent before providing special education and related services in the IEP.

However, the federal special education law and regulations do not require the parent to give consent to subsequent IEPs. Consent requirements vary from state to state, so you need to review your state special education regulations.

You may revoke your consent for special education services, in writing, at any time.

Although federal law does not require the parents' signatures, having parents sign the IEP has benefits:

- A signed IEP documents who attended the meeting. If the IEP is not signed, the school must find another way to document the members who attended the meeting.
- An IEP signed by the parent usually indicates that you consent to the IEP. Look at the IEP to see if your signature is consent or simply attendance. If you do not consent to the IEP, write your concerns adjacent to your signature. After the IEP, write a more detailed follow-up letter.
- An IEP signed by the school representative provides you with a record of the services the school agreed to provide. Even if school staff does not sign the IEP, the school must provide all services called for in the IEP.[4]

I don't agree that the proposed IEP is sufficient, but it's better than nothing. The team says I have to "take it or leave it!" Can I allow the school to implement parts of the IEP while we continue to negotiate the issues where we don't agree?

Yes. Allowing the school to implement acceptable parts of the IEP is a good idea.

The school may not draw a line in the sand or say that you must "take it or leave it." The school may not use your refusal to consent to one service or activity to deny other services, benefits, or activities.[5]

Parents and school staff are equal participants in IEP meetings. IEP meetings allow you and school personnel to discuss your child's needs and how these needs will be addressed. You and the school will decide on the services your child needs and will receive.

If you cannot agree on part of a proposed IEP, consider a trial period to implement parts of the IEP. You and the school should agree on a timeframe for the trial period and document this in the IEP.

Establish a time and method to evaluate the plan, measure progress, and decide if the plan is working. A trial period allows everyone to take part in the decision-making process.[6]

Can a foster parent or surrogate consent to the IEP?

Yes. The law defines a "parent" as:[7]

- Natural, adoptive, and foster parents (unless prohibited by state law) and guardians
- An individual who acts in the place of natural or adoptive parents (i.e., a grandparent, step-parent, or other relative) and with whom the child lives
- An individual who is legally responsible for the child's welfare
- An individual assigned to be a surrogate parent

Unless prohibited by state law, foster parents may serve as parents in special education decisions. Check your state law and regulations about the status of foster parents.

My daughter has made little or no progress in special education. Can I revoke consent for her to receive special education services?

Yes, you may revoke your consent for special education services **in writing** at any time. In your letter, explain the reasons why you are revoking consent for special education services.[8]

After you revoke consent, the school will not continue to provide your daughter with special education and related services.

Parent Participation

Schools must do all they can to ensure that parents participate in the IEP process.

Schools are responsible for scheduling meetings, informing parents about meetings, and for making good faith efforts to ensure that one or both parents are able to attend. The school must also ensure that parents can understand the proceedings.

Advocate's TIP

Good Advocates ...

- Facilitate the IEP proccess
- Know the child and understand the disability
- Work to reduce barriers between the parent and school
- Admit mistakes and apologize
- Hone their listening skills to a sharp edge
- Learn the art of negotiation
- Know the special and general education law, and the interrelationships with other laws
- Recognize the importance of ethical behavior in their practice
- Treat others the way they would like to be treated

by Pat Howey, Advocate

How will I know when an IEP meeting is scheduled and who will attend?

The school must take steps to ensure that one or both parents attend each IEP meeting.

The school must provide you with a notice that includes the purpose, time, and location of the meeting and who will attend the meeting. The notice will also inform you about your right to invite other people who have knowledge or special expertise about your child.[9]

The school says the IEP team only meets during school hours. I can't leave work during school hours but I can attend a meeting after school. Should the school comply with my request for an after-school IEP meeting?

Yes. Many parents are in the same boat – they cannot leave work during the day or cannot attend a meeting during the day. As the parent, you have a right to participate in meetings to develop your child's IEP.

The school is required to take steps to ensure that you can attend any meeting about your child's special education program. For example, the school must notify you about a meeting early so you can make arrangements to attend. The school is also required to schedule meetings at a mutually agreed upon time and place.[10]

Write a letter to the school. Describe your situation. Request that the meeting time be changed. Include several dates and times when you can be available.

I want to help develop my child's IEP but I can't attend the IEP meeting. What can I do?

If you cannot attend a scheduled meeting, you need to let the school staff know that you want to attend. You and the school need to look for a mutually agreed upon time and place. If you still cannot solve the problem, the school must use other methods, including telephone and conference calls, to ensure that you can participate in developing your child's IEP.[11]

I attend IEP meetings with parents who are not fluent in English. Should the school provide an interpreter so the parents know what is happening and can participate in decision-making?

Yes. The parental participation section of the law requires schools to take action to ensure that parents understand what is happening during the IEP meeting. This includes arranging for an interpreter for parents who are deaf or hard of hearing, and for parents whose native language is not English.

Send a short letter to the school and advise them about the need to obtain an interpreter. Do this as early as possible so the school has time to find a qualified interpreter.[12]

Are parents allowed to have copies of assessments and evaluations before the IEP meeting?

Yes. Parents often say that the school refused to provide evaluations and assessments before meetings. You want to participate meaningfully in your child's IEP meetings. To participate meaningfully, you need copies of your child's evaluations before the IEP meeting. The evaluations that determined eligibility are free.[13]

Your child's psycho-educational evaluation

and other tests are education records. The federal special education regulations state that if a parent requests their child's education records, "The agency must comply with a request without unnecessary delay and before any meeting regarding an IEP..."[14] You may be charged a fee for the copies of the records but not a charge to search for the records.[15]

Advocate's TIP

If the school did not provide evaluations or proposed IEP goals before the IEP meeting and this affected your ability to participate in the IEP process, reschedule the meeting.

The law is clear.

Parents are full participating members of their child's IEP team. You cannot be a full participating IEP team member if you do not receive key information about your child before the meeting.

by Anne Eason, Esq.

Can the school have an IEP meeting without me?

Yes, in very limited circumstances. Before the school can have an IEP meeting without you, they must try to schedule the meeting at a time and place that is convenient for you and other team members. If the school cannot persuade you to attend the IEP meeting, the team can meet without you.

If the team holds an IEP meeting without you, it is required to keep a record of attempts to arrange a meeting with you at a mutually agreed upon time and place. This includes:

- Records of telephone calls made or attempted and your response
- Copies of correspondence sent to you and your response
- Detailed records of visits made to your home or place of employment and the results of these visits[16]

Is the school required to provide me with a copy of my child's IEP?

Yes. The school must provide you with a copy of your child's IEP at no cost.[17] If your child's IEP is revised or amended, you are entitled to a copy, but you may need to request it.

When I asked for a copy of my child's IEP at the end of the meeting, the team leader said they would send me a "clean copy" in a few days. I want a copy of the IEP we agreed upon during the meeting. What can I do?

You should get a copy of your child's IEP right away. There is no reason for delay.

If the school wants to send you a "clean copy," thank them, but make it clear that you want a copy of the original IEP before you leave the meeting. Ask them to send you the "clean copy" when it's available. When you get the clean copy, compare it to the original.

If you do not get a copy of your child's

IEP, write a short polite letter to request a copy. Explain that the school did not provide an original copy in spite of your request at the meeting.

In Summation

In this chapter, you learned about your parental role and parental consent. You learned why you should be an active participant in developing your child's IEP.

In the next chapter, you will begin learning how to write an IEP. You will learn about using present levels of academic achievement and functional performance to devise measurable IEP goals.

Endnotes

1. 34 C.F.R. § 300.9
2. Regulations adopted, effective December 31, 2008 at www.wrightslaw.com/idea/law/FR.v73.n231.pdf
3. 20 U.S.C. § 1414(a)(1)(D); 34 C.F.R. § 300.300(b)(1)
4. Appendix C, Question #29
5. 34 C.F.R. § 300.300(d)(3)
6. Appendix C, Question #35
7. 20 U.S.C. § 1401(23); 34 C.F.R. § 300.30
8. Regulations adopted, effective December 31, 2008 at www.wrightslaw.com/idea/law/FR.v73.n231.pdf
9. 34 C.F.R. § 300.322(b)(1)
10. Commentary in 71 FR at 46678; C.F.R. § 300.322(a)(1)
11. 34 C.F.R. § 300.322(c)
12. 34 C.F.R. § 300.322(e)
13. 34 C.F.R. § 300.306(a)(2)
14. 34 C.F.R. § 300.613(a); Commentary in 71 FR at 46645
15. 34 C.F.R. § 300.613; 34 C.F.R. § 300.617
16. 34 C.F.R. § 300.322(d)
17. 34 C.F.R. § 300.322(f); 34 C.F.R. § 300.324(a)(6)

4 Present Levels, Measurable IEP Goals, Special Education Services

- Present Levels of Academic Achievement and Functional Performance
- Measurable IEP Goals
- Short-Term Objectives and Benchmarks
- Statement of Special Education Services
- Physical Education and Adapted PE
- Is Your Child's IEP Individualized?

In this chapter, you will learn how to use present levels of academic achievement and functional performance to write measurable IEP goals. You will learn when IEPs must include short-term objectives and/or benchmarks.

You will also learn about requirements for special education services and physical education services, and how the IEP team determines the services your child needs.

At the end of the chapter is a checklist that you can use to determine if your child's IEP is individualized.

The Individuals with Disabilities Education Act describes how to develop IEPs. The child's IEP team **shall** consider:

- The child's strengths
- The parents' concerns for enhancing the child's education
- Results of the initial evaluation or most recent evaluation of the child
- The child's academic, developmental, and functional needs[1]

At the beginning of the IEP process, the team must determine your child's present levels of academic achievement and functional performance. The team also needs to know how the child's disability affects his involvement and progress in the general education curriculum. The IEP must:

- Be based on your child's present levels of academic achievement and functional performance
- Include measurable annual goals to meet all your child's needs that result from the disability
- Enable your child to be involved and make progress in the general education curriculum
- Describe how the school will measure your child's progress and how the school will inform you about progress
- Meet other educational and non-educational needs[2]

Present Levels of Academic Achievement and Functional Performance

The term "performance" describes what a child can do. The present levels of academic achievement and functional performance (sometimes called PLOP or PLAAFP) are objective data that describe what your child knows and is able to do. Collecting baseline data is the starting point to create accurate, current, and educationally useful present levels.

What are present levels of academic achievement and functional performance?

Present levels describe your child's unique needs that result from his disability. Present levels are data that describe your child's strengths, challenges, and needs.

The present levels of academic and functional performance include baseline data. Before an IEP team can develop measurable IEP goals that monitor the child's progress, the team must collect baseline data.

Present levels of academic achievement include subjects like reading, math, and spelling. Present levels of functional performance include non-academic and functional areas like communication, fine motor skills, behavior and social skills, and daily life activities.[3]

Where does the IEP team get the information for present levels of academic achievement and functional performance?

Present levels of academic achievement and functional performance are based on data from objective assessments. Other sources of information may be informal assessments and observations by parents and teachers.[4] If the child has earlier IEPs, his progress toward goals in the prior IEPs should be reviewed.

As a parent, you observe your child and have important information about his strengths and needs. Your child's teachers and related service providers collect data about how your child functions in school settings.

Do all IEPs include present levels of academic achievement and functional performance?

Yes. The team must collect baseline data that describes your child's present levels of performance. The team uses this baseline data to write measurable IEP goals that will allow you and the school to monitor your child's progress.

The team should also develop strategies to insure that your child is involved in and making progress in the general education curriculum, as the law requires. In addition, the team may use this information to develop accommodations and/or modifications to the curriculum.[5]

What are "functional skills?"

Functional skills include daily living activities—social skills, mobility skills, employment skills, and skills that increase your child's independence.[6]

Must all IEPs include functional goals?

No. After the IEP team determines your child's present levels of functional performance, the team may decide that your child does not have functional needs that should be addressed in the IEP.

Our IEP team wants to use data from two-year-old assessments for the present levels in this year's IEP. Should the IEP team use current information for the "present levels" statements?

Yes. Your child's present levels of academic achievement and functional performance should use baseline data about your child's academic and functional levels now, in the present.

In developing an IEP, the team must ensure that data is collected to measure and monitor your child's progress often (i.e., weekly, biweekly, monthly). The purpose of frequent monitoring is to assess your child's progress and evaluate the effectiveness of instruction.

How can I get the IEP team to use accurate information for the present levels of achievement and performance sections of the IEP?

Ask questions - 5 W's + H + E questions.

When you ask 5 W's + H + E questions, you frame your questions so they begin with one of these words: What, Why, When, Who, Where, How, and Explain.

Assume your child is in fifth grade. Her reading skills are at the second or third grade level. Here are some questions you may ask the team about her IEP:

- What are my child's present levels of academic achievement in reading (baseline)? Writing? Spelling? Math?
- What is the school doing to ensure that my child learns how to read at grade level?
- How will the team monitor my child's progress?
- How and when will the school provide information about my child's progress?
- When will my child be able to read at grade level?
- What services does my child need to read at grade level by next year?
- When will we know if the team's plan is working?
- What will the team do if my child does not make adequate progress under the current plan?

Assume your child is in the eleventh grade. Here are some questions you may ask about his present levels of functional performance.

- Can my child read a job application? Can he complete a job application without assistance?
- Can my child read the driver training manual? Did he pass the driving test without assistance?
- Can he balance a checkbook?
- Can he read a map? A bus schedule?
- Does he ask for and understand directions?

Present Levels Statements Checklist

1. Do the Present Levels Statements include current, measurable data that correspond with measurable IEP goals? _____ (Yes, No, Not sure)

2. Do the Present Levels Statements include baseline data that you and the school can use to monitor your child's progress toward the IEP goals? _____ (Yes, No, Not sure)

3. Does the IEP describe what your child is doing now, including:

_____ Strengths

_____ Needs related to the child's disability

_____ Your parental concerns

- Does he use the Internet to do research?
- How does he interact with other people? Does he ask a sales clerk for the price of an item? Can he make a purchase without help?
- Can he order food from a menu?

Measurable IEP Goals

Measurable goals cannot be broad statements about what a child will accomplish in a year. Measurable IEP goals must use baseline data from the child's present levels of academic achievement and functional performance. Measurable goals should be written so the child's progress is clear and measurable.

You have learned that your child's IEP must identify and meet all your child's needs that result from the disability. The IEP team must also determine how your child's disability affects his involvement and progress in the general education curriculum. These are key factors to keep in mind when developing an appropriate IEP.[7]

I'm confused about measurable goals.

Measurable IEP goals describe what your child can reasonably be expected to accomplish in areas of need within a specified period of time. "Measurable" means you can count, observe it, and document it.

Which of these two goals is measurable?

> Owen will improve his reading skills.
>
> Given second grade material, Owen will read a passage of text orally at 110-130 wpm with random errors as measured by the Gray Oral Reading Test (GORT).

Measurable goals allow parents and teachers to observe whether a child is making progress, regressing, or staying the same. When the team develops clear measurable IEP goals, parents and school staff know when the IEP needs to be modified and adjustments to instruction made.

Measurable IEP goals target the child's unique needs. They do not describe the general education curriculum. They do not list what a child is expected to learn in every content area.

SMART IEPs

Chapter 12 in ***Wrightslaw: From Emotions to Advocacy, 2nd Edition*** will teach you how to write SMART goals.

You will learn how to use baseline levels of performance to write SMART goals. SMART goals are **S**pecific, **M**easurable, use **A**ction words, **R**ealistic, and **T**ime-limited.

The goals in my child's IEP are not measurable: "Evan will improve in reading" and "Evan will improve in mathematics." How do you make goals measurable?

Your child's IEP must include a statement about how your child's progress toward meeting the goals will be measured.[8] There are several ways to make a goal measurable.

- You can specify performance at a grade or age level on objective tests.
- You can indicate a rate. (i.e., 3 out of 4 times, 5 minutes out of every 10 minutes)
- You can use a standardized assessment, criterion-referenced test, or progress monitoring.

At a minimum, measurable goals include the following:

- What is the expected change in the child's performance or behavior?
- What needs are being targeted? (i.e., skill, area of knowledge or understanding, behavior)
- What criteria will be used to measure progress or growth? (i.e., how much, how often, to what level of proficiency)[9]

My child has behavior problems. How do you make behavior goals measurable?

You make behavior goals measurable by describing the factors surrounding the behavior. These factors include:

- Precipitating events ("when asked to work independently")
- Environmental factors ("when dealing with female authority figures")
- Results of the behavior ("removal from the classroom increases this negative behavior")
- Other observable patterns ("after lunch," "always on the playground," "in math class")

Many IEP goals that are developed to address behavior are not measurable. For example, "to listen attentively" and "to use time constructively" are not measurable. You cannot observe if a child is "listening attentively" or "using time constructively."

You can revise these goals to make them measurable. You can observe how often the child is "paying attention" during a specified period of time and develop goals to improve in this area. You can revise the time-management goal to "increase the # of minutes (or other unit of time) that the child is on task." You can get baseline information for the present levels by observing the amount of time the child is on and off task.[10]

The IEP team must specify the criteria that will be used to measure progress on behavior goals. This involves identifying how well and over what period of time your child must perform a behavior before the goal is met.

Steps to Write a Measurable IEP Goal

1. Collect baseline data that will be used to write the child's present levels.
2. Select skills and behaviors that will be targeted. Clearly define the observable behavior that will change.
3. Establish performance criteria / how progress will be measured (i.e., speed, accuracy, frequency, duration, etc.)
4. Write the goal.

My child's IEP has academic goals but no functional goals. Should all IEPs include functional goals?

No. After the IEP team describes the present levels of functional performance, the team may conclude that your child does not have functional needs. If your child does not have a weakness in daily living activities, social skills, mobility skills, employment skills, or any other skills necessary for independence, your child's IEP may not include functional goals.

My child has social skills deficits but is doing fine academically. Can the IEP have goals that address her social skills deficits, but no academic goals?

Yes. The IEP team must look at your child's unique academic, developmental, and functional needs. This includes her needs for social and independent living skills. Her deficits in social skills should be addressed in her IEP. If she is doing well academically, then her IEP may not include academic goals.

Does the IEP team have to consider my concerns about my child's special education program?

Yes! In developing your child's IEP, the team must consider your concerns for enhancing your child's education.[11] The team must also consider your child's strengths, results of the initial evaluation or most recent evaluation, and your child's academic, developmental, and functional needs.[12]

The team says they do not write IEP goals for general education classes like pre-calculus and humanities courses. Is this correct?

Is your child's performance in these classes affected by his disability? If the disability does affect his performance in these classes, the team should write IEP goals to address these issues.

If a qualified student with a disability requires supplementary aids and services to participate in regular education classes, then the school cannot deny the needed aids and services if the student is in an accelerated class or program.[13]

If the child does not need direct assistance in regular education classes, he may still need accommodations like extended time on tests. Classroom and testing accommodations must be written into the IEP.

Can you give me examples of good IEP goals?

This is the most frequently asked question about IEPs. The short answer is "no." IEP goals must be individualized to the unique needs of a particular child. An IEP goal that is appropriate for one child will not be appropriate for a child who has different needs.

IEP goals should be **S**pecific, **M**easurable, use **A**ction words, **R**ealistic, and **T**ime-limited.

At the last IEP meeting, the team cut my child's IEP from ten goals to

four goals. Is there a legal limit to the number of goals in the IEP?

No. The law does not limit the number of goals in an IEP. Your child's IEP must address all academic, functional, and developmental needs that result from your child's disability.

An IEP is unlikely to be appropriate if it sets arbitrary limits on the number of goals. Some parents come to IEP meetings with long lists of goals in many areas. It's a good idea to prioritize goals, and decide what goals need to be tackled first.

Is the school responsible for ensuring that my child reaches all the goals in the IEP?

No. The IEP is not a contract that guarantees outcomes. The IEP describes the child's needs and the individualized instruction that provides educational benefit that the school agrees to provide.[14]

Short-Term Objectives and Benchmarks

My child has multiple disabilities and takes alternate assessments. Should her IEP include short-term objectives and/or benchmarks?

Yes. The IEPs of children who take alternate assessments must include short-term objectives and/or benchmarks.[15] Short-term objectives and benchmarks are steps that measure the child's progress toward the annual goals in the IEP. When written correctly, short-term objectives allow you and your child's teachers to monitor your child's progress frequently.

Measurable IEP Goals Checklist

1. Does each IEP goal describe what your child will learn or be able to do in a specific period of time (i.e., one semester, one academic year?)
_____ Does each goal meet a need that results from your child's disability?

_____ Will the goal enable your child to be involved in and make progress in the general curriculum?

2. Is each IEP goal:

_____ Specific

_____ Measurable

_____ Active

_____ Relevant

_____ Time-limited (can be achieved within the term of the IEP)

3. Does each goal meet a need identified in the present levels of performance? _____

Statement of Special Education Services

After the IEP team determines the child's present levels and develops measurable goals, the team will make decisions about special education services, related services, and supplementary aids and services.

The law defines "special education" as "specially designed instruction, at no cost to the parents, to meet the unique needs of a child with a disability."[16] Specially designed instruction should meet the child's unique needs and ensure the child's access to the general curriculum. Specially designed instruction includes adapting the content, methodology, or delivery of instruction.

Should my child's IEP include all the services he needs?

Yes. The IEP must include all special education services, related services, and supplementary aids and services your child needs, and the school will provide. The law requires these services to be based on peer-reviewed research "to the extent practicable."[17]

Services in the IEP may include:

> **Special education services:** specially designed instruction designed to meet your child's unique needs.[18]
>
> **Related services:** services your child needs to benefit from special education (i.e., speech language therapy, occupational therapy, physical therapy, nursing services).[19]
>
> **Supplementary aids and services:** services and supports your child receives in general education classes and other settings so your child can be educated with children who are not disabled.[20]

What is peer-reviewed research?

Peer review is the process of submitting an author's research or ideas to others who are experts in the same field.

Peer-reviewed research generally refers to research that is reviewed by qualified and independent reviewers to ensure that the quality of the information meets the standards of the field before the research is published.[21]

Should my child's IEP include specific information about the services he will receive?

Yes. The IEP must include the projected date to begin services, and the frequency, location, and duration of services.[22] The amount of time for each service must be stated in the IEP so the school's commitment of resources is clear to you, and to the teachers and related service providers who will implement the IEP.[23]

Our state wants IEP teams to develop IEPs based on state standards. I am concerned that standards-based or state aligned IEPs do not address a child's weakness in the basic skills or reading, writing, arithmetic, and spelling, and are not individualized to meet the child's needs.

Standards-based or state aligned IEPs move away from creating individualized IEPs for children with disabilities.

The purpose of IDEA is "to prepare" the child "for further education, employment, and independent living" so children are "prepared to lead productive and independent adult lives" to develop "economic self-sufficiency."

For this purpose to be achieved, children with disabilities must learn basic reading, writing, arithmetic, and spelling skills. The IEP needs to address the child's deficiencies, and close the achievement gap between kids with disabilities and nondisabled kids.

After our school changed their service delivery system, they do not specify the amount of services in IEPs. Can they do this?

No. The school must comply with the legal requirements for IEPs. The service delivery system is irrelevant.

As noted earlier, the IEP must include the projected date to begin services, and the frequency, location, and duration of these services. The amount of special education or related services should be stated as a specific number of minutes rather than a range (e. g, speech therapy to be provided three times a week for 30-45 minutes per session).[24]

The school says my child's IEP is based on "what we have available." Is this right?

No. The IEP team is required to develop an IEP that meets all your child's needs, regardless of "what is available" at the school. Your child's IEP must be individualized. "What we have available" usually refers to one-size-fits-all programs that are not individualized to meet a child's unique needs.

Physical Education and Adapted PE

If your child has a disability and an IEP, the school must provide physical education as part of the child's special education program. Many children benefit from adapted physical education.[25]

My child has a disability and an IEP. Is she entitled to physical education?

Yes. The IDEA requires that students with disabilities be provided with physical education. The law defines Physical Education as the development of:

- Physical and motor skills
- Fundamental motor skills and patterns
- Skills in aquatics, dance, and individual and group games and sports (including intramural and lifetime sports)[26]

Physical education includes special physical education, adapted physical education, movement education, and motor development.

What is adapted physical education?

Adapted physical education (APE) is physical education that is modified to meet the unique needs of a child who has motor and/or developmental delays. In APE, the instructor adapts or modifies the curriculum, task, equipment, and/or environment so the child can participate in physical education.[27]

Because physical education is a required component of special education, the child's physical education teacher should be included as a member of the IEP team.

My child has diabetes and an IEP. Can he benefit from adapted PE?

The answer depends on his needs. In many cases, the PE teacher will assess the child. This assessment will determine your child's present levels of performance, strengths and weaknesses in motor skills, sports, and fitness.

In general, children with diabetes benefit from aerobic exercise. The IEP may include an aerobic exercise program that is tailored to his needs.

Note: You need to consult with your child's health care provider before beginning a new fitness program.

Is Your Child's IEP Individualized?

When you answer these questions, you will know if your child's IEP is individualized, as the law requires.

- Does the IEP include accurate information about your child's present levels of academic achievement and functional performance?
- Does the IEP identify all your child's needs that result from the disability?
- Does the IEP include measurable goals?
- Are the measurable goals based on your child's present levels of academic achievement and functional performance?
- Does the IEP describe how and when the school will measure your child's progress toward the goals?
- Does the IEP specify when you will receive reports on your child's progress toward the annual goals?
- Does the IEP include a statement of the special education services, related services and supplementary aids and services that the school will provide?
- Does the IEP allow your child to make progress in the general curriculum, and participate in extracurricular and other nonacademic activities?
- Does the IEP include an explanation of the extent to which your child will be educated with children who are not disabled?
- Does the IEP include the projected date services will begin? Frequency? Location and duration of services?

In Summation

In this chapter, you learned that you begin the IEP process by identifying the child's present levels of academic performance and functional performance. You learned about IEP goals and how to make goals measurable.

You also learned that physical education is a required component of special education and how adapted PE can help children with disabilities.

You learned that IEPs must be individualized to the unique needs of each child with a disability.

In the next chapter, you will learn about related services and supplementary aids and services.

Endnotes

1. 20 U.S.C. § 1414(d)(3)(A)

2. 20 U.S.C. § 1414(d)

3. 20 U.S.C. § 1414(d)(1)(A)(i)(II), ***Wrightslaw: Special Education Law, 2nd Edition***, p. 99, footnote 74-75

4. Appendix A, Question #1

5. Appendix A, Question #1

6. Commentary in 71 FR at 46661

7. 20 U.S.C. § 1414(d)(1)(A)(i)(I)(aa)

8, 20 U.S.C. § 1414(d)(1)(A)(i)(III); 34 C.F.R. § 300.320(a)(3)(i)

9. www.naset.org/760.0.html

Additional Resource: www.specialed.us/issues-IEPissues/writingiep/WritingIEPs.htm

10. www.wrightslaw.com/blog/?p=35

11. 34 C.F.R. § 300.324(a)(1)(ii)

12. 20 U.S.C. § 1414(d)(3)(A); 34 C.F.R. § 300.324(a)(1)

13. ***Access by Students with Disabilities to Accelerated Programs*** at www.ed.gov/about/offices/list/ocr/letters/colleague-20071226.html

14. Appendix C, Question #60

15. 20 U.S.C. § 1414(d)(1)(A)(i)(I)(cc); 34 C.F.R. § 300.320(a)(2)(ii)

16. 20 U.S.C. § 1401(29)

17. 20 U.S.C. § 1414(d)(1)(A)(i)(IV)

18. 20 U.S.C. § 1401(29)

19. 20 U.S.C. § 1401(26)

20. 20 U.S.C. § 1401(33)

21. ***Wrightslaw: Special Education Law, 2nd Edition***, p. 100, footnote 79

22. 34 C.F.R. § 300.320(a)(7)

23. 34 C.F.R. § 300.320(a)(7)

24. Appendix A, Question #35

25. 20 U.S.C. § 1401(29)

26. 34 C.F.R. § 300.39(b)(2)

27. Adapted Physical Education National Standards (APENS) at www.apens.org/

5 Related Services, Supplementary Aids & Services

- Related Services
- Transportation
- Support and Training for School Personnel
- Parent Counseling and Training
- Supplementary Aids and Services
- Extracurricular and Nonacademic Services in the IEP

In this chapter, we will look at related services and supplementary aids and services. You will learn that your child's IEP may include support and training for school personnel and parents.

You will also learn about extracurricular and nonacademic services.

Related Services

What are related services?

Related services are the developmental, corrective, and supportive services your child needs to meet the measurable goals and receive a free, appropriate public education (FAPE).

Related services include, but are not limited to:

- Speech-language and audiology services
- Interpreting services
- Psychological services and social work services in schools
- Counseling services and rehabilitation counseling
- Physical therapy, occupational therapy, orientation and mobility services
- Recreation and therapeutic recreation
- Early identification and assessment of disabilities in children
- School health and school nurse services
- Medical services for diagnostic or evaluation purposes
- Parent and teacher training

What information about related services should be included in my child's IEP?

Your child's IEP should include the frequency, duration, location, and projected dates for each related service. This includes:

- When the related service will begin
- How often the child will receive the related service(s) (number of times per day or week)
- How long each session will last (number of minutes)
- Where the related service will be provided (i.e., in the general education classroom or special education resource room)
- When the related service will end[1]

The frequency and duration of related services should be specific, not stated as a range.[2]

The model IEP form published by the U.S. Department of Education (2006) provides the format to record required information about related services.

TIP: Does your child's IEP say PT 2x week "per school calendar?" Most school holidays fall on Monday or Friday. You do not want to lose those therapy days that will not be made up due to school holidays. To avoid this problem, select Tuesday, Wednesday, or Thursday for your child's therapy.

If you cannot get services on these days, be sure to state in the IEP that the missed therapy sessions will be made up before the end of the school year or through extended school year services (ESY).

Can a child with a disability be eligible for speech-language services, but not for special education services?

Yes. Some children receive related services like speech therapy and physical therapy but are not eligible for special education services.

Model IEP Form

Requires the projected date for the beginning of the services and modifications and the anticipated frequency, location, and duration of special education and related services and supplementary aids and services and modifications and supports. 34 C.F.R. § 300.320(a)(7)

Service, Aid or Modification	Frequency	Location	Begin date	Duration

You will find the complete Model IEP Form from the US Department of Education at www.ed.gov/policy/speced/guid/idea/modelform-iep.pdf

Many states include speech-language therapy and other related services under the definition of "special education."[3] "Special education" is defined as "specially designed instruction, at no cost to the parents, to meet the unique needs of a child with a disability… ."[4]

Are there limits on the speech, physical, and occupational therapy a child can receive?

No. All decisions about special education services and related services should be individualized and based on the child's unique needs.

My child was born deaf and has a cochlear implant. When I asked the school to monitor the device to ensure it is working, they said the law does not allow them to do this because the cochlear implant is a medical device. Does the law prohibit this?

No. Serving children with cochlear implants is essentially the same as serving children with hearing aids. The school is responsible for checking the external components of cochlear implants and hearing aids to ensure that they are working.[5]

Teachers and related services providers should check your child's externally worn speech processor to make sure it is turned on, the volume and sensitivity settings are correct, and the cable is connected, just as they check to make sure a child's hearing aid is functioning properly.

Allowing a child to sit in a classroom when the child's hearing aid or cochlear implant is not functioning excludes that child from receiving an appropriate education.[6] See Chapter 7, Special Factors in the IEP, to learn about services for children who are deaf or hard of hearing.

One of my students received a cochlear implant. As a teacher, what can I do to help her?

As a teacher, you have an important role in providing services and supports to your student with a cochlear implant.

With a younger child or a child who recently received a cochlear implant, the teacher is often the first to notice changes in the child's perception of sounds or sounds the child is missing. You may notice a lack of attention or frustration in communicating. These changes may indicate that the device needs to be remapped. Discuss your observations with your student's parents. A specially trained professional adjusts or remaps the device.[7]

My child has an insulin pump. Is the school responsible for maintaining or replacing this device?

No. An insulin pump is a surgically implanted device. The school is not responsible for maintaining or replacing surgically implanted devices. However, the school is responsible for checking a surgically implanted device to determine if the external component of the device is turned on and working.

Transportation

If the IEP team decides that your child needs transportation to benefit from special education, the team should include transportation as a related service in the IEP.

Do all children with disabilities have a right to transportation as a related service?

No. Only children with disabilities who need transportation services and have these services noted in their IEPs receive transportation services. If your child does not have transportation services in the IEP, your child will not receive transportation services.

If the school provides transportation for nondisabled children, it must provide transportation to children with disabilities.

If the school does not provide transportation to nondisabled children, the team will make decisions about transporting your child on a case-by-case basis.[8]

My child has an orthopedic impairment and an IEP. She uses a power wheelchair. She needs ramps to get around the school and school grounds safely. Is the school required to provide transportation and assistance?

Yes. Your child has a disability and needs assistance. Transportation and assistance should be provided as a related service to help her:

- Travel to and from school
- Travel between schools
- Get around inside the school buildings
- Get around school grounds[9]

Her IEP should include her need for ramps and a school bus with a wheelchair lift as related services. If the school uses a bus with a lift, your child should be able to ride the bus with other neighborhood children.

My son has autism and an IEP. His communication skills are limited and he is easily distracted. His judgment is poor. I'm afraid to let him walk to the school bus stop. Can I ask the school to provide special transportation?

Yes. You and the other IEP team members decide whether your child needs special transportation services in his IEP. The school must arrange for transportation if the team decides that your child's disability prevents him from:

- Using the same transportation as children who are not disabled
- Getting to and from school the same way as children who are not disabled

Before the IEP meeting, write a letter to the IEP team leader. Describe your child's disability and special transportation needs. Explain that it is not safe for him to travel to and from the bus stop by himself.

Ask the team to include his need for door-to-door transportation as a related service in his IEP.

Support and Training for School Personnel

Your child's IEP must include a statement of modifications or supports that will be provided to school personnel when appropriate.

Teachers and other school personnel receive support and training so their students with disabilities can be educated with children who are not disabled. They also receive training so children with disabilities can meet their IEP goals, make progress in the general education curriculum, and participate in extracurricular and nonacademic activities as members of the school community.[10]

Training as a related service in a child's IEP does not include the general in-service training that is available to school staff.[11]

My child has autism and an IEP. He gets overwhelmed when riding the bus. Can the bus driver get training in how to manage his behavior problems?

Yes. The need for training and support applies to all school personnel. School bus drivers are expected to handle children with different needs related to cognitive, behavioral, and medical conditions. A school bus driver may need training in behavior management techniques for children with autism and emotional disturbances.

The bus driver may also need training from physical and occupational therapists about how to position a medically fragile child, or training from the school nurse about how to transport a child with health impairments.

If your child has transportation needs, ask the school bus driver to join the IEP team.[12]

Support and training for teachers and other school personnel must be written in the child's IEP. For more about IEPs for children with behavior problems, see Chapter 7 about Special Factors in the IEP.

My child is eligible for special education due to a traumatic brain injury. He has an aide, but still struggles in class. His teacher says he doesn't need more help, he would do fine in school if he only applied himself. Why don't teachers understand how this condition affects his ability to perform?

Your child's teachers more than likely need information about his disability and effective instructional techniques for a child with TBI. The school may need to bring in an outside expert in traumatic brain injury to train the teachers and provide consultation services about how this injury affects your son.

If your child's teacher needs professional development and consultation services, she should receive these services from an expert in the field, the school psychologist, special education teacher, behavior interventionist, or other specialists.

Consultation includes, but is not limited to:

- Training in how to teach children who have challenging problems
- Mentoring from a staff member who has expertise in teaching children with these issues

Parent Counseling and Training

My preschool child receives speech therapy at school. I would like to supplement the speech therapist's services with receptive and expressive language exercises at home. Can the school provide me with training to do this?

Parents can receive training as a related service. When you know what your child is working on in speech therapy, you can practice and reinforce the receptive and expressive language exercises at home.

You need to make sure that parent training as a related service is written into your child's IEP.

My child has ADHD and has trouble completing homework. He gets frustrated and angry. I want to help him but I don't know how. Can I receive training to help my child?

Yes. As a parent, you can learn effective strategies to help your child. The law ensures that you have meaningful opportunities to participate in your child's education at school and at home.[13]

Parent training helps parents understand the special needs of their child. This training may provide parents with information about child development. It also helps parents acquire skills that allow them to help implement their child's IEP or Individualized Family Service Plan (IFSP).[14]

Counseling is another related service that may be available for you if your child has behavior problems that interfere with his ability to learn. You can receive mental health counseling and/or family therapy to help you handle his behavior. You can receive counseling to learn communication and behavior management skills. You may want to consult with school personnel so you and the school are using consistent approaches to deal with behavior issues. These services may help your child meet his IEP goals.

As with all special education and related services, the IEP team makes decisions about parent counseling and training. The team must write parent training or counseling in your child's IEP for you to receive this as a related service.

My child has an orthopedic impairment and mobility problems. The IEP team wants to eliminate mobility goals from his IEP because they do not have enough occupational and physical therapists. Do I have to let them do this?

No! The school must provide your child with a free, appropriate public education (FAPE). This includes the physical therapy and occupational therapy he needs. The responsibility to provide the services your child needs does not end because of financial hard times, personnel shortages, or staff absences.

If the school cannot or did not hire enough therapists to provide the related services your child needs, the school can contract with qualified providers from other agencies or from the private sector.[15] Your district may use federal, state, local, and private sources of support to provide special education and related services.[16]

My child is partially paralyzed and attends mainstream classes. He requires a ventilator to breathe and a person who can attend to his physical needs at school. The school says these are medical services and they are not required to provide them. Is this correct?

No. The school must provide all special education services, related services, and supplementary aids and services your child needs to receive a free, appropriate public education. Tending to your child's ventilator and his physical needs are nursing services. Because your child needs nursing services to attend school and receive a free, appropriate education, the school is required to provide these related services. Period!

The school must also monitor and maintain medical devices that children need for health and safety. In addition to hearing aids and cochlear implants, this includes other medical devices that help with bodily functions, breathing, and eating.

Rule on Health and Nursing Services: U.S. Supreme Court

The U.S. Supreme Court has issued two decisions on these services.

When health services are necessary for FAPE: *Irving School District v. Tatro* (1984)

When nursing services are necessary for FAPE: *Cedar Rapids v. Garret F.* (1999)

Chapter 11 and 12, ***Wrightslaw: Special Education Law, 2nd Edition***

Supplementary Aids and Services

Many children with disabilities need supplementary aids and services so they can participate in academic and extracurricular activities with their classmates. Supplementary aids and services are provided in regular education classes and other education settings so children with disabilities can be educated with children who are not disabled.[17]

When is a child with a disability eligible for supplementary aids and services?

All children with disabilities are eligible for supplementary aids and services. Supplementary aids and services enable children with disabilities to participate in academic, nonacademic, and extracurricular activities with their classmates who are not disabled.

Who decides what supplementary aids and services a child will receive?

Your child's IEP team decides what supplementary aids and services your child needs. All decisions about the supplementary aids and services a child needs should be individualized to meet the child's unique needs.

When and where should a child receive supplementary aids and services?

A child may receive supplementary aids, services, and supports in regular education classes, nonacademic settings, and extracurricular activities.[18]

Assume your child has a disability that includes severe muscle weakness and deficits in fine motor skills. Your child plans to attend college and needs to take chemistry in high school. When the class conducts lab experiments, your child may need help from an aide or paraprofessional to complete the chemistry experiments safely.

Extracurricular and Nonacademic Services in the IEP

Nonacademic Services and Extracurricular Activities

- Sports
- Counseling
- Health services
- Recreation
- School newspaper and literary magazines
- Band
- Chorus
- Special interest groups and clubs

Can my child's IEP include extracurricular activities and after-school programs?

Yes. Extracurricular activities enhance your child's life as a member of the school community. When IDEA was reauthorized in 2004, Congress amended the law to ensure that children with disabilities could participate in extracurricular activities and other nonacademic activities.[19]

Should supplementary aids and services be listed in my child's IEP?

Yes, the IEP must list the supplementary aids and services your child needs and the school will provide. Your child needs these aids and services to participate in activities with classmates who are not disabled. The school must ensure that your child receives all supplementary aids and services listed in the IEP.[20]

The IDEA states that supplementary aids and services must be based on peer-reviewed research "to the extent practicable."[21]

Here are examples of supplementary aids and services:

- **Supports to address environmental needs:** preferential seating; planned seating on the bus, in the classroom, at lunch, in the auditorium, and in other locations; changed room arrangement
- **Levels of staff support:** consultation, stop-in support, classroom companion, one-on-one assistance; type of personnel support: behavior specialist, health care assistant, instructional support assistant
- **Planning time:** collaboration needed by staff
- **Child's specialized equipment needs:** wheelchair, computer, software, voice synthesizer, augmentative communication device, utensils/cups/plates, restroom equipment
- **Pacing of instruction:** breaks, more time, home set of materials
- **Presentation of subject matter:** taped lectures, sign language, primary language, paired reading and writing
- **Materials:** scanned tests and notes into computer, shared note-taking, large print or Braille, assistive technology
- **Assignment modifications:** shorter assignments, taped lessons, instructions broken down into smaller steps, allow student to record or type assignment
- **Self-management and/or follow-through:** calendars, teach study skills
- **Testing adaptations:** read test to child, modify format, extend time, provide private testing space
- **Social interaction support:** provide Circle of Friends, use cooperative learning groups, teach social skills
- **Personnel training**[22]

Recommended Resources

Comprehensive Listing of Supplementary Aids and Services

www.ped.state.nm.us/seo/library/qrtrly.0204.lre.handouts.pdf

In Summation

In this chapter, you learned about related services and supplementary aids and services – what they include and how the IEP team makes decisions about the services your child needs.

In the next chapter about developing your child's IEP, you will learn about the requirements that schools advise parents about their child's progress during the school year. You will also learn about accommodations, modifications and alternate assessments in the IEP.

Endnotes

1. 34 C.F.R. § 300.320(a)(7)
2. Appendix A, Question #35
3. 34 C.F.R. § 300.8(a)(2)
4. 34 C.F.R. § 300.39(a)(1)
5. Commentary in 71 FR at 46571
6. Commentary in 71 FR at 46571
7. Commentary in 71 FR at 46570-1
8. www.nichcy.org/EducateChildren/IEP/Pages/RelatedServices.aspx
9. 34 C.F.R. § 300.34(c)(16)
10. 34 C.F.R. § 300.320(a)(4)
11. Commentary in 64 FR (1999) at 12593
12. www.nhtsa.dot.gov/people/injury/buses/UpdatedWeb/topic_9/page1.html
13. 20 U.S.C. § 1400(c)(5)(B)
14. 34 C.F.R. § 300.34(c)(8), Commentary in 71 FR at 46573
15. www.fape.org/pubs/fape-33.pdf
16. Appendix A, Question #31
17. 20 U.S.C. § 1401(33); 34 C.F.R. § 300.42
18. 20 U.S.C. § 1401(33); 34 C.F.R. § 300.42
19. 34 C.F.R. § 300.117
20. Commentary in 71 FR at 46589
21. 34 C.F.R. § 300.320(a)(4)
22. *A Sampling of Supplemental Supports Aids & Services*" developed by the New Mexico Public Education Department and available at: www.ped.state.nm.us/seo/library/qrtrly.0204.lre.handouts.pdf.

6 Progress, Accommodations, Modifications, and Alternate Assessments

- Notifying Parents About Their Child's Progress
- Accommodations & Modifications
  - In the Classroom
  - On Tests
- Alternate Assessments
- Methodology in the IEP

In this chapter, you will learn about the requirements for measuring your child's progress toward the IEP goals. You will learn when the school will provide you with periodic reports of your child's progress toward the annual goals.

You will also learn about accommodations in the classroom and on state proficiency tests, and requirements about alternate assessments.

Notifying Parents About Their Child's Progress

How will I know if my child is making progress? Is this stated in the IEP?

Yes. Your child's IEP must describe how your child's progress toward the annual goals will be measured and when you will receive progress reports. The school may issue periodic progress reports quarterly (four times a year) or when report cards are issued.[1]

Ask your child's teachers and service providers how and when they will measure your child's progress. You may ask:

- How often will you measure my child's progress?
- What tests or assessments will you use to measure my child's progress?
- How often will you communicate with me about my child's progress or lack of progress?

Can the school district issue a report card that includes information about my child's special education program? For example, can the report card refer to my child's IEP?

Yes. The purpose of report cards is to inform parents about their child's progress or achievement in classes. A report card can indicate that your child is receiving special education services if it includes information about your child's progress in classes.[2]

Should my child's report card assign grades based on grade level standards?

Yes. If your child attends regular education classes that use grade level standards to measure student progress, the school will assign grades to all students enrolled in these classes.

Recommended Resources

National Center on Student Progress Monitoring
http://www.studentprogress.org

National Center on Response to Intervention
http://www.rti4success.org

My child's IEP states that progress will be reported by "teacher observation." I want objective information about my child's progress. Any suggestions?

You bring up an important point.

When a child's progress is monitored by subjective "teacher observations" and "teacher-made tests," parents do not have objective data about their child's progress toward the goals in the IEP. You are being asked to rely on subjective beliefs and/or opinions. You should be concerned about this practice.

There are several ways to measure progress:

- Frequency (e.g., 9 out of 10 trials)
- Duration (e.g., for 20 minutes)
- Distance (e.g., 20 feet)
- Accuracy (e.g., 90% accuracy)

The IEP team should define a period of time for a skill or behavior to be measured:

- Number of days (e.g., over three consecutive days)
- Number of weeks (e.g., over a four week period)
- Occasions (e.g., during Math and English classes, on six consecutive occasions)

If you have questions about your child's progress, write a polite note to the teacher or related service provider. Ask to see the objective data that documents your child's progress.

What is progress monitoring?

In progress monitoring, the teacher uses short tests to evaluate your child's progress in specific areas. The teacher tests your child often - every week or two. Progress monitoring tells the teacher what the child has learned and what still needs to be taught.

The teacher creates progress graphs that show the child's progress toward the IEP goals. You may receive copies of these progress graphs every few weeks. If you do not, write a short letter to request your child's progress graphs.

Can the school use progress monitoring in the IEP?

Yes. Progress monitoring is a scientifically based practice used to assess your child's academic progress and evaluate the effectiveness of instruction. Progress monitoring can be used with one child or an entire class.

Since state assessments measure academic skills, how will we know if our child is making progress in developmental and functional skills?

Good question. There are several ways to measure progress on developmental and functional goals.

In interpreting test data, the law requires the IEP team to include information about aptitude and achievement.[3] Achievement is not limited to academics. Teachers often use assessments that are part of developmental and functional curricula to measure student achievement.

The IEP team can measure progress on developmental and functional skills by writing measurable IEP goals. The team can also compare results from earlier evaluations to results from current evaluations.

For students with severe disabilities, goals must be written so the child's progress can be tracked with benchmarks or short-term objectives.

IEP Progress Reports **Checklist**

1. Does the IEP state how your child's progress toward the IEP goals will be measured? _____

2. Will your child's progress on IEP goals be reported the same as progress is reported to parents of nondisabled children? _____

3. Will the IEP Progress Report indicate whether your child is making sufficient progress toward the IEP goal? _____

Accommodations & Modifications

The purpose of special education is to prepare students with disabilities "for further education, employment, and independent living."[4]

If the school does not teach your child how to read, write, spell, and do arithmetic, your child will not be prepared for adult roles or life after school.

What is the difference between accommodations and modifications?

Accommodations are intended to help your child work around the disability and demonstrate what he has learned. Accommodations do not change a test or assignment in a significant way. Your child is expected to learn the same information. For example, a child who has fine motor problems and difficulty with handwriting may be allowed to type answers on a test or assignment.

Appropriate accommodations attempt to level the playing field by teaching compensatory strategies and techniques. An accommodation may provide additional time so your child can demonstrate what she has learned.

Unlike accommodations, modifications change the nature of an assignment or test. Modifications make assignments and tests easier. For example, a modification may require a child to answer only half the questions on a test.

Accommodations and Modifications in the Classroom

Common accommodations in the classroom include:

- Providing a tutor
- Assigning a note-taker for a child who cannot listen and take notes at the same time
- Permitting computer use for a child who has illegible handwriting
- Tape recording class lectures
- Allocating extra time to complete tests
- Taking tests in a quiet room

Common modifications in the classroom include:

- Providing shorter, modified assignments; assignments replaced by easier assignments
- Reducing work to what is relevant to a child
- Omitting higher math facts, simplifying other tasks
- Reducing number of concepts taught
- Giving different tests

My child is mainstreamed in regular classes. How can we ensure that he has the classroom accommodations he needs?

Your child needs accommodations that allow him to overcome obstacles caused by his disability.

You and other members of the IEP team need to identify your child's strengths and weaknesses. These strengths and weaknesses will help the team decide on accommodations that are appropriate for your child. If accommodations are individualized and appropriate, he should be able to participate and make progress in the general education curriculum.

Your child's IEP team must include at least one regular education teacher. Regular education teachers are knowledgeable about the general education curriculum. They should know appropriate accommodations that will help your child learn and make progress.

> **Warning!** Some schools use accommodations and modifications instead of teaching children the skills they need to master. Without these skills, children will not become independent, self-sufficient members of society. Before you consent to modifications, think carefully about the purpose of the modification. Ask how the proposed modification will allow your child to learn essential skills. The purpose of modifications is not higher grades, but learning.

Accommodations and Modifications on Tests

Accommodations on tests are intended to provide children with a chance to demonstrate what they know. When a child with a disability does not receive appropriate accommodations, a test often measures the impact of a child's disability, not what the child knows.

Accommodations on tests may change how a test is administered. They do not substantially change what a test measures.

Common test accommodations include:

- Testing in a quiet place for students who are easily distracted
- Extended time on tests
- Different test formats (e.g., presentation format or response format)

My child has a disability and an IEP. Is he eligible for accommodations on high-stakes tests?

The federal education laws establish high standards and high expectations for all children – including children with disabilities.

The standard is mastery of the state curriculum. The laws require children with disabilities to participate in state and district assessments. Your child's IEP team will decide which state assessment is appropriate.[5]

Your child's IEP must include a statement of the accommodations and/or modifications on state and district tests. States must allow accommodations in test materials and procedures, scheduling, and setting. Check your state special education regulations.

Alternate Assessments

Alternate assessments are designed for children with disabilities whose cognitive impairments may prevent them from attaining grade-level achievement standards.

Alternate assessments must be aligned with the general curriculum standards established for students in the state.

Who decides if my child will take an alternate assessment?

If the IEP team determines that your child will not participate in a particular state or district assessment of student achievement, the team must state why the assessment is not appropriate for your child and how your child will be assessed.[6]

My child has a severe disability. Is he exempt from taking state and district assessments?

No. All children must take state and district assessments. Decisions about whether the child needs to take an alternate assessment will depend on the child's unique needs, not on the category of the child's disability. Most children with disabilities are able to keep up with their peers academically and take standardized tests successfully as long as they receive appropriate specialized instruction.

Participation in Assessments Checklist

1. Did the IEP team discuss whether your child will participate in state and local assessments? _____
2. Did the IEP team discuss whether your child will participate in standardized district assessments? _____
3. If your child needs accommodations to participate in standardized assessments, are these accommodations listed in the IEP? _____
4. If your child will take alternate assessments, did the team discuss:

_____ Why the standardized assessment is not appropriate?

_____ How the child will be assessed through alternate means?

Many children with disabilities do not qualify for special education. These children are able to participate on regular standardized tests.

Methodology in the IEP

My child was evaluated and diagnosed with dyslexia and dysgraphia. The psychologist advised that she needs a reading program based on Orton-Gillingham principles. The IEP team said the school chooses the methodology. Is this true?

The law does not require your child's IEP to include educational methodology.

The position of the U.S. Department of Education is that including methodology in a child's IEP is an IEP team decision. If the IEP team decides that your child needs a specific method to receive a free, appropriate public education, the instructional method may be included in the IEP.[7]

> *In light of the legislative history and case law, it is clear that in developing an individualized education there are circumstances in which the particular teaching methodology that will be used is an integral part of what is 'individualized' about a student's education and, in those circumstances will need to be discussed at the IEP meeting and incorporated into the student's IEP.*[8]

Are reading specialists required to use research based reading programs with their special education students?

"States, school districts, and school personnel must…select and use methods that research has shown to be effective, to the extent that methods based on peer-reviewed research are available."[9]

States must ensure that school personnel are appropriately and adequately prepared and trained. Teachers must have the content knowledge and skills to teach children with disabilities. This includes the use of research based instructional practices.

School districts must ensure that their personnel have the knowledge and skills to improve the academic achievement and functional performance of children with disabilities.[10]

In Summation

In this chapter you learned the requirements for measuring your child's progress toward the annual goals and how and when the school must provide you with periodic reports of progress.

You learned the difference between accommodations and modifications. You also learned requirements for alternate assessments.

In the next chapter you will learn about special factors that IEP teams must consider in developing your child's IEP.

Endnotes

1. 20 U.S.C. § 1414(d)(1)(A)(i)(III); 34 C.F.R. § 300.320(a)(3)
2. *Questions and Answers on Report Cards and Transcripts For Students with Disabilities* www.ed.gov/about/offices/list/ocr/letters/colleague-qa-20081017.html
3. 34 C.F.R. § 300.306(c)
4. 20 U.S.C. § 1401(d)
5. 34 C.F.R. § 300.320(a)(6)
6. 20 U.S.C. § 1414(d)(1)(A)(VI); 34 C.F.R. § 300.320(a)(6)
7. Commentary in 71 FR at 46665
8. *Methodology in the IEP* by Pam Wright and Suzanne Whitney at www.wrightslaw.com/info/iep.methodology.htm
9. Commentary in 71 FR at 46665
10. 20 U.S.C. § 1412(a)(14), 34 C.F.R. § 300.156

7 Special Factors in IEPs

- Behavior Problems
- Limited English Proficiency
- Blind or Visually Impaired
- Deaf or Hearing Impaired
- Communication Problems

In this chapter, you will learn about five special factors that IEP teams must consider when developing a child's IEP.[1]

You will learn what the IEP team must consider when developing an IEP for a child who has behavior problems.

You will learn that if a child has limited English proficiency, the team must consider the child's language needs and provide services to meet these needs.

If a child is blind or visually impaired, the team must decide about teaching the child to use Braille.

If a child is deaf or hearing impaired or has communication problems, the IEP team must meet the child's communication and language needs. To learn about the school's responsibilities to children who need assistive technology devices and services, see Chapter 8.

Behavior Problems

If your child's behavior prevents him or other children from learning, the IEP should include goals to address these problem behaviors. The team should consider positive behavioral interventions and supports (PBIS) and other strategies to change the child's behavior.

Research demonstrates that positive behavioral interventions and supports are effective in dealing with behavior that is dangerous, disruptive, impedes learning, and leads to social exclusion. PBIS are used to create positive behavioral change in children with developmental disabilities, autism, emotional and behavioral disorders.[2]

What is a functional behavioral assessment?

A functional behavioral assessment (FBA) identifies the purpose a behavior serves for a child.

In a functional behavioral assessment an individual who has been trained to collect and analyze data will observe the child in different settings. The evaluator or behavior analyst looks for events that immediately precede the problem behavior (triggers or antecedents) and events that immediately follow the problem behavior (rewards or consequences).

Assume a child has learned that screaming is an effective way to avoid or escape unpleasant tasks. Putting the child in timeout would provide what the child wants (to avoid the task) and is likely to make the problem worse.

Without an adequate functional behavioral assessment, the IEP team, teachers, parents, caregivers, who work with your child will not know the function of the child's screaming. If they do not have this information, they are likely to select interventions that are not appropriate.

What happens in a functional behavior assessment?

The evaluator or behavior analyst will observe your child in different settings (i.e., the classroom, cafeteria, playground). The evaluator will also gather reports from your child's teachers and others who work with your child. The evaluator may also interview you and your child.

The evaluation process includes these steps:

- Identify the behavior that needs to change
- Collect data on the behavior
- Develop a hypothesis about the reason for the behavior
- Develop an intervention to help change the behavior
- Collect data on the intervention (time, scope, duration)
- Use the data to evaluate the effectiveness of the intervention

After the functional behavioral assessment is completed, the IEP team will review this information and develop a plan to deal with your child's problem behaviors. If the IEP team decides to use behavior interventions, these interventions must be included in your child's IEP.[3]

When should the IEP team refer a child for a functional behavioral assessment?

When your child's behavior has a negative impact on his ability to learn or his classmates' ability to learn, the IEP team should refer him for a functional behavioral assessment. If the school changes your child's placement for disciplinary reasons, the IEP team should complete a functional behavioral assessment.[4]

> **Recommended Resources**
>
> **Addressing Behavior Issues in the IEP**
>
> OSEP National Technical Assistance Center on Positive Behavioral Interventions and Supports
> www.pbis.org
>
> Your State Coordinator: Contact your regional or state PBIS coordinator for technical support or questions concerning the implementation of PBIS.
> www.pbis.org/links/pbis_network/default.aspx
>
> www.nichcy.org/educatehildren/IEP/pages/special-factors.aspx

An IEP team member observed my child in the classroom, then wrote a functional behavioral assessment. Is this sufficient?

Maybe. First, an evaluator or behavior analyst directly observes and measures your child's behavior in different environments. The evaluator should focus on the environment where your child's misbehavior occurs. If your child's behavior problems occur in the classroom only, it makes sense to observe the child in the classroom and other school settings.

After the assessment, a team of people who are knowledgeable about your child will develop a behavior intervention plan (BIP).

What is a behavior intervention plan?

A behavior intervention plan (BIP) or positive intervention plan is designed to teach and reinforce positive behavior. A behavior intervention plan may include:

- Skills training to increase appropriate behavior
- Changes in the classroom and other environments to reduce or eliminate problem behaviors
- Strategies to replace problem behaviors with appropriate behaviors
- Supports for your child to use the appropriate behaviors
- Data collection to monitor your child's progress

The process of conducting a functional behavioral assessment and developing a behavior intervention plan differs from state to state. Please check your state special education regulations to learn the procedures in your state.

If the school removes your child from his current placement as a discipline procedure, the team should complete a functional behavioral assessment and develop a behavior intervention plan to address the behavior problem so it does not recur.[5]

Monitoring Progress in a Behavior Intervention Plan

In progress monitoring school personnel collect data about the child's progress frequently. Progress monitoring data is documented.

Are the anticipated outcomes being met? Are the placement and services appropriate?

The behavior intervention plan is modified often, based on progress monitoring data. Is the intervention effective?

The school communicates with the parents frequently when developing and implementing the behavior intervention plan.

For more read, ***Functional Behavioral Assessments: Creating Positive Behavior Intervention Plans*** published by the Center for Effective Collaboration and Practice at http://cecp.air.org/fba/default.asp

My child has autism. The school had him arrested for assault. Although the charges were dismissed, I am afraid this will happen again. What can I do?

If the school had your child arrested, the problem behaviors must be serious. The IEP team must develop a plan to address these behaviors.

Write a letter to the special education director with copies to the principal and the head of your child's IEP team. Describe the incident that led to the arrest. Request a functional behavioral assessment. (See the sample letter.) Request an IEP meeting to review the functional behavioral assessment and develop positive interventions and strategies to address the behavior problems. The IEP team needs to monitor the effectiveness of the plan.

Limited English Proficiency

Children must be proficient in English before they can become proficient in other subjects. If a child does not read, write, or speak English well, the IEP team needs to ensure that the child's language needs are met.

I adopted a child from another country. His English is limited. He has a disability and an IEP. Should he receive special education in English or in his native language?

The IEP team makes decisions about how your child's limited English affects his need for special education and related services. The IEP team must make decisions about whether:

- He will receive instruction in English and/or in his native language so he can participate in the general curriculum
- His special education and related services will be provided in his native language

Sample Letter to Request Functional Behavioral Assessment and Positive Behavior Support Plan

Martha Johnson
204 Stingray Road
Middlesex, CA
313-652-7795
September 12, 2009

Mr. Charles Martin, Special Education Director
Applewood School District
1415 Hartfield Drive
Middlesex, CA 88888

Re: Emily Johnson (DOB: 09/12/98), Applewood Elementary School

Dear Mr. Martin:

My child, Emily Johnson, attends Applewood Elementary School. I believe that Emily's behavior is interfering with her ability to learn and to reach her IEP goals. My concerns are:

- She does not know how to respond constructively to name-calling or teasing
- She is not cooperative in groups
- She cannot distinguish between socially acceptable and unacceptable behaviors
- She does not recognize situations when she needs to exercise self-control
- She does not know how to cope with stress-provoking situations she cannot avoid
- She does not understand the consequences of appropriate and inappropriate expressions of emotions

Please consider this letter my formal request for and consent for the school district to provide Emily with a functional behavioral assessment as required by the Individuals with Disabilities Education Act (IDEA). I understand that a positive behavior support team will review the assessment and develop an appropriate behavior intervention plan.

I expect to be included in the assessment and to participate in developing the behavior intervention plan. Please provide me with copies of all FBA results when they are available to you. Please expedite this request as Emily has been suspended from school three times for a total of 9 days this year.

Thank you for giving this request your immediate attention. I look forward to working with you. If you have questions about my request, please call me at work (313-989-3434) or at home (313-652-7795) after 6 p.m., or you may email me at marthajohnson@middlesexca.com.

Sincerely,

Martha Johnson

Drafted courtesy of Calvin and Tricia Luker, Respect ABILITY Law Center

- He needs tutoring in English as a service in his IEP

Before making these decisions, the IEP team must obtain an assessment of your child's English proficiency. This assessment should include objective data about your child's reading, writing, speaking, and understanding skills.

What should be included in his IEP?

The IEP must specify his need for instruction in English and/or his native language, and his need for English language tutoring.

If your child needs test accommodations because of limited English proficiency (e.g., increased time, translating directions into his native language, etc.), these accommodations must be written in his IEP.

My child has a disability and limited English. Is he entitled to services from a speech-language pathologist?

Maybe. Whether your child is eligible for services from a speech-language pathologist depends on his needs. You may need to request these services.

Limited English Proficiency (LEP) Checklist

For a child with limited English proficiency to be educated effectively, the IEP team needs to address these issues:

1. Has the child's primary language of communication been considered? __Yes__No
2. Does a member of the IEP Team have expertise about the child, knows how language develops, and knows strategies to use when educating a child with limited English proficiency? __Yes__ No
3. Does the IEP Team have access to accurate data that is unbiased? __Yes__ No
4. Does the assessment use a variety of methods and environments? __Yes__ No
5. Is the child's progress toward mastery of English being monitored with objective tests? __Yes__No
6. Has the dominant language in the home been considered? __Yes__No
7. Is an interpreter for the parents and the student present at the IEP meeting? __Yes__No
8. Do the goals specify the language that will be used and the person measuring outcomes? __Yes__No

For a comprehensive checklist for a child with limited English proficiency, go to Special Factors at www.nde.state.ne.us/sped/technicalassist/iepproj/factors/lep.html or www.nichcy.org/Pages/resourceD-4.aspx

Speech-language pathologists are excellent resources for children who have limited English. They can suggest ways to modify the classroom and curriculum, depending on the child's proficiency in English. They may also:

- Help the classroom teacher find ways to take the child's language skills into account during instruction
- Help the classroom teacher understand differences in communication styles of children with limited English skills
- Help children who are eligible for speech language services learn the structure, meaning, and use of English
- Teach the child's parents how to use language stimulation activities[6]

Blind or Visually Impaired

A visual impairment is defined as "impairment in vision that, even with correction, adversely affects a child's educational performance." The term includes partial sight and blindness.[7]

The visual abilities of children with visual impairments differ. One child may have no functional vision and may learn through the tactual sense, including Braille. Another child may be able to read and write print materials if they are modified. The IEP team must decide how the child learns and if the child needs to learn Braille.

Because children's needs change often, the IEP team should review your child's visual abilities often. The learning medium may need to be changed too.[8]

One of my students with an IEP has very poor vision. She needs eyeglasses, but her family can't afford to purchase them. Since she cannot learn without glasses, is the school responsible for providing them?

Eyeglasses and hearing aids are assistive technology devices. Does your student need eyeglasses to participate in special education, related services, or supplementary aids and services? If the answer is "yes," the school must provide the eyeglasses (or hearing aids) at no cost to the child's parents.

The child may use school-purchased assistive technology devices like eyeglasses or a hearing aid at home or in other settings if the IEP team decides that she needs to use the device to receive FAPE.[9]

What does the law say about instruction in Braille?

If your child is blind or visually impaired, you can request that your child receive instruction in Braille. The IEP team must provide instruction in Braille unless the IEP team determines that Braille is not appropriate for your child.

Before the IEP team can decide if instruction in Braille is or is not appropriate, they must conduct an evaluation of your child's reading and writing skills, needs, and appropriate reading and writing media. Your child's future needs for instruction in Braille should also be evaluated.[10]

Visual Impairment Checklist

For a child with a visual impairment to be educated effectively, the IEP team needs to address these issues:

1. Has the student received a functional vision evaluation? __Yes__No

__ Student's vision is so limited a functional vision evaluation would not be appropriate

2. Has the student received a learning media assessment? __Yes__No

3. Has the student received a recent clinical low-vision assessment? __Yes __No

__ Student's vision is so limited low vision clinical examination is not appropriate

4. Does the student's visual condition indicate:

__ A progressive loss of vision?

__ Stability at the current level?

__ Unpredictability that will be followed by a possible decrease in vision?

__ A temporary condition that is expected to improve?

5. Is there a medically diagnosed expectation of visual deterioration in adolescence or early childhood? __Yes__No

6. Does the student qualify for instruction in a new primary reading and writing medium because the student cannot use the current medium? __Yes__No

7. Will the student receive instruction in Braille? (The IEP team must provide for instruction in Braille unless the IEP team determines, after evaluation of the child's reading and writing skills, that instruction in Braille is not appropriate.) __Yes__No

8. If instruction in Braille is not appropriate, which primary and secondary learning media has been selected for this student?

___Primary Secondary
___Large Print
___Regular Print
___Regular Print with an optical device
___Closed circuit television
___Recorded
___Individual is a non-reader

For a comprehensive checklist for a child with a visual impairment, go to Special Factors at www.nde.state.ne.us/sped/technicalassist/iepproj/factors/bli.html or www.nichcy.org/Pages/resourceD-5.aspx

Your child's IEP should include a statement like "Because of the student's visual impairment, reading materials, assignments, and tests need to utilize Braille."

My child needs textbooks in Braille. Is the school responsible for ensuring that he has textbooks in Braille at the beginning of the school year?

Yes. The school must have an IEP in place for each child with a disability at the beginning of the school year.[11] The IEP must include the special education services, related services, and supplementary aids and services that meet your child's unique needs and provide him with a free, appropriate public education (FAPE).

If the IEP specifies that your child will have textbooks in Braille, the school must provide these textbooks at the beginning of the school year. If the school does not provide textbooks at no cost to you, they are not providing your child with FAPE.

My child has a cortical visual impairment (CVI). How will the school know how she learns?

The IEP team must evaluate your child's reading and writing skills and determine her needs. This evaluation should determine appropriate reading and writing media for your child. The IEP team should use the results of this evaluation to decide if your child needs instruction in Braille.[12]

Some states require IEP teams to conduct additional assessments of children who are blind or visually impaired. A Functional Vision Assessment (FVA) can determine how to adapt and modify testing and instruction to meet the unique needs of a child with a vision impairment.[13]

A Learning Media Assessment (LMA) identifies the best reading format for your child (i.e., print, Braille, audio, combination). A Learning Media Assessment helps the IEP team make other decisions about how to educate your child.

Check your state special education regulations to learn the requirements in your state.

Recommended Resources

"The Learning Media Assessment" published by the Perkins School for the Blind.
www.perkins.org/scout/literacy-and-braille/learning-media-assessment.html

When evaluating a child who is blind or visually impaired, the evaluator needs to be familiar with the National Instructional Materials Accessibility Standard (NIMAS). This new legal provision improves access to instructional materials for children with disabilities. See Chapter 8 about Assistive Technology.

Deaf or Hearing Impaired

I am a special education teacher and have a deaf-blind student in my class. At the last IEP meeting, I advised the team that she needs an interpreter. The supervisor refused to consider my request. Doesn't the law say that the district must provide an interpreter if the child needs this service?

Yes. As a deaf-blind student, your student has unique needs. The school is required to provide the services she needs. Interpreting services are related services. The federal special education regulations include "special interpreting services for children who are deaf-blind" as an interpreting service.[14]

You may also want to review the questions and answers about related services in Chapter 5.

My child was born deaf. At the last meeting, we discussed his needs but did not develop an IEP. What services should the school provide?

The first step is to get a comprehensive psycho-educational evaluation of your child. The evaluation should include information about how your child's communication needs change in different environments (e.g., classroom, cafeteria, gym, computer lab, home, community). For a child who has a hearing impairment, the IEP team must consider the child's:

- Academic level
- Language and communication needs, including direct instruction in his communication mode
- Opportunities to communicate with classmates and teachers
- Needs for assistive technology devices and services[15]

After the IEP team identifies your child's needs, the team will develop measurable IEP goals to meet these needs. The measurable IEP goals are based on your child's present levels of academic achievement and functional performance. The IEP should also include measurable goals to meet your child's communication needs.

As the parent member of the IEP team, you need to educate the team about how your child learns and communicates. For example, describe how your child communicates with family and friends.

My daughter is in the deaf/hearing impaired program at school. She is active in sports. I enrolled her in a summer basketball camp sponsored by the school to improve her skills. The school refuses to provide interpreting services because the camp is not required. Is this right?

Your child's IEP team makes decisions about the special education services, related services, and supplementary aids and services your child needs. Supplementary aids and services allow children with disabilities to participate in academic, nonacademic and extracurricular activities with their classmates who are not disabled.

You are a member of your daughter's IEP team. Write a letter to the chairperson of the team. Describe your daughter's passion for basketball and her need to improve team skills. Ask the IEP team to revise her IEP to include interpreting services for basketball camp. These services must be described in her IEP.

Communication & Language Needs Checklist

For a child with communication and language needs to be educated effectively, the IEP team should ensure:

The communication plan
____ Is addressed by all members of the IEP Team.
____ Is completed during the IEP meeting.
____ Provides information regarding the student's mode of communication (receptively and expressively).
____ Addresses the student's language and communication needs.
____ Addresses the student's academic level.
____ Addresses the student's full range of needs.
____ Describes opportunities for direct communication with peers and professionals.
____ Describes opportunities for direct instruction in the child's language and communication mode.
____ Incorporates all of this information into the development of the IEP.

For a comprehensive checklist for a child with communication and language needs, go to Special Factors at www.nde.state.ne.us/sped/technicalassist/iepproj/factors/deaf.html

Communication Problems

Communication problems have a negative impact on a child's ability to learn. Communication also plays a key role in interpersonal relationships. A child who has communication problems usually has social and behavior problems that interfere with learning.

My child has autism and is nonverbal. He gets angry and frustrated because he cannot communicate what he wants and needs. I want the school to teach him a way to communicate. The school claims that he cannot be taught. What can I do?

Your nonverbal child with autism must have a way to effectively communicate.

Speech is a way to communicate that takes place in a social context. For children with autism, communication and social skills are interdependent.

Before the IEP team can develop an appropriate communication program, they must obtain a comprehensive assessment of the child's communication abilities. Your child needs services from a specialist who can teach him a functional method of communication. An appropriate intervention program includes several elements:

- Develops communicative intent
- Establishes an efficient and appropriate way (form) to communicate
- Expands the range of communicative functions or purposes

- Develops the ability to respond to and initiate communication
- Develops strategies to repair breakdowns in communication[16]

My daughter has Rett Syndrome. She is high functioning but she cannot speak. I want her IEP to have communication goals. The school says she doesn't need communication goals because she can't speak.

Most children with Rett Syndrome have severely impaired expressive language skills. While children with Rett Syndrome often lose the ability to speak, they do not lose the desire and need to communicate.

The IEP team is required to consider your child's communication needs. When your child has severe language and communication problems, the goal is to increase her ability to communicate. She needs direct instruction in a mode of communication. A speech therapist may work with an occupational therapist to improve her ability to communicate.

Since your child cannot speak, the IEP team must also consider her needs for assistive technology. The team should schedule an assistive technology evaluation to identify her needs and how to meet these needs. Brilliant physicist, Stephen Hawking, cannot speak. He communicates through assistive technology.

She may benefit from low-tech devices like picture boards, head pointers, and switches to activate a computer program. She may need high-tech devices like voice output devices and a computer so she can access the general education curriculum.

Please review the information about assistive technology devices and services in Chapter 8.

Recommended Resources

Intervention for Students With Communication Disorders
Intervention decisions must be based on a thorough understanding of speech and language development and the processes of communication.
www.asha.org/docs/html/GL2000-00053.html

Autism Interventions and Strategies for Success: Developing Expressive Communication Skills for Non-verbal Children With Autism by Susan Stokes, Autism Consultant,
www.specialed.us/autism/nonverbal/non11.htm

In Summation

In this chapter you learned about the five special factors IEP teams must consider in developing and revising IEPs. If your child has one or more of these special factors, the IEP team must address them in the child's IEP.

In the next chapter, you will learn how assistive technology can help your child meet academic and functional goals. You will also learn about the new national standards for accessible print materials.

Endnotes

1. 20 U.S.C. § 1414(d)(3)(B); 34 C.F.R. § 300.324(a)(2)
2. OSEP National Technical Assistance Center on PBIS at www.pbis.org
3. 34 C.F.R. § 300.324(a)(2)(i); ***Discipline for Children With Disabilities: Answers to Questions About Discipline Under IDEA*** from the Office of Special Education Programs www.wrightslaw.com/advoc/articles/discipline_faqs_osep.htm
4. 20 U.S.C. § 1415(k)(1)(D)
5. 34 C.F.R. § 300.530(d)
6. ***Guidelines for the Roles and Responsibilities of the School-Based Speech-Language Pathologist*** at www.asha.org/docs/html/GL2000-00053.html
7. 20 U.S.C. § 1401(3); 20 U.S.C. § 1401(30); 34 C.F.R. § 300.8(13)
8. ***Services to Blind or Visually Impaired Students*** at www.nde.state.ne.us/sped/technicalassist/iepproj/factors/bli.html
9. 20 U.S.C. § 1412(a)(1); 20 U.S.C. § 1412(a)(12)(B)(i); 34 C.F.R. § 300.105; Commentary in 71 FR at 46581
10. 34 C.F.R. § 300.324(a)(2)
11. 20 U.S.C. § 1414(d)(2)(A)
12. 20 U.S.C. § 1414(d)(3)(A)(iii)
13. The definition of related services at 34 C.F.R. §300.34 includes orientation and mobility services for blind and visually impaired children at 34 C.F.R. § 300.34(7)
14. 20 U.S.C. § 1401(26); 34 C.F.R. § 300.34(c)(4)
15. 20 U.S.C. § 1414(d)(3)(B)(iv) and (v)
16. ***Developing Expressive Communication Skills for Non-verbal Children With Autism*** by Susan Stokes, Autism Consultant, under a contract with CESA 7 and funded by a grant from the Wisconsin Department of Public Instruction. www.specialed.us/autism/nonverbal/non11.htm

8 Assistive Technology (A.T.)

- A.T. Devices and Services
- A.T. Evaluations and Plans
- Universal Design for Learning

In this chapter, you will learn about using technology to assist your child in school and at home. Assistive technology (A.T.) includes "devices" and "services."

Assistive technology helps children with disabilities learn and meet their IEP goals.

Assistive technology has other benefits. With appropriate assistive technology, children function more independently and their confidence increases.

Assistive technology is **not** a substitute for teaching the child to read and write.

Because assistive technology has so many benefits, the law requires IEP teams to consider the assistive technology needs of all children with disabilities.[1]

In this chapter, you will also learn about the new national standards for accessible print materials.

> *"Teaching students to read by the end of 3rd grade is the single most important task assigned to elementary schools."*
> American Federation of Teachers
>
> After 3rd grade, schools should continue to provide research-based reading instruction, but if a child is still struggling, he will need technology at school and home to access the general curriculum (e.g., social studies and science) in electronic formats.

A.T. Devices and Services

Many children with disabilities have difficulties with reading, writing, and math. Some children have problems with vision, hearing, listening and/or communicating. Others have physical, mobility, and motor problems.

Assistive technology helps children use their strengths to compensate or "work around" weaknesses caused by the disability.

The law requires schools to use assistive technology devices and services "to maximize accessibility for children with disabilities."[2]

The IEP team makes decisions about assistive technology devices and services. All decisions must be individualized to meet the child's unique needs. The IEP team must answer these questions for a child who has an IEP:

- Does this child need assistive technology to meet the academic and functional goals in the IEP?
- Does this child need assistive technology in the regular education class and/or special education setting?

Children with disabilities who struggle to learn often become dependent on their parents and teachers for help with schoolwork. If the IEP team selects assistive technology based on a child's unique needs, the child can be more confident and independent.

What is an assistive technology device?

The law defines an assistive technology device as "any item, piece of equipment, or product system, whether acquired commercially off the shelf, modified, or customized, that is used to increase, maintain, or improve the functional capabilities of a child with a disability."[3]

Many people think "assistive technology" is computer hardware, software, and electronic devices. Assistive technology goes far beyond computers, and includes thousands of high-tech and low-tech tools. A.T. devices include communication devices, visual aids, wheelchairs, dictation software, text readers, computerized speaking devices, pencil grips, and slant boards.

When thinking about A.T. devices or services, keep your child's needs in mind.

What are her strengths? Areas of weakness? What does she need help to do? Where and how will she use the technology?

Assume your child is deaf or hearing impaired. A.T. devices for your child may include:

- Alerting Devices: Signal Lights, Ring Enhancers, Sound Activated Lights
- Assistive Listening Devices & Systems: FM and Sound Field FM Systems; Classroom Amplification
- Captioning: Open, Closed, Realtime
- Telecommunication Devices: Amplified phones; TTY/TDD phones

Assume your child has a specific learning disability. Children with learning disabilities have weaknesses in the academic areas of reading, writing, spelling, and/or math. Many children with learning disabilities also have problems with listening, attention, organization, and/or memory.

A.T. devices for children with learning disabilities include:

- Text-to-speech (reading) and Word Prediction (writing) software
- Alternative keyboards
- Audio books and publications
- Graphic organizers and outlining
- Information and data managers
- FM listening systems
- Portable word processors and proofreading programs
- Speech recognition programs; speech synthesizers and screen readers
- Talking spell checkers, electronic dictionaries

Recommended Resources

The Essential Guide to Assistive Technology

Marshall Raskind, Ph.D. provides an overview of assistive technologies and advice about selecting appropriate tools for children with learning problems.

www.greatschools.net/LD/assistive-technology/parents-guide-to-assistive-technology.gs?content=784

If your child needs assistive technology devices, they must be listed in the IEP. The IEP should include a statement like this: "Because Chris has fine motor problems, she requires assistive technology devices including pencil grips and a tape recorder, in school and at home."

If your child needs assistive technology, you need to discuss assistive technology services with the IEP team.

What are assistive technology services?

If your child needs assistive technology, the IEP team must also consider assistive technology services.

These services allow the child, family, and educators to learn to use assistive technology devices and tools.

Assistive technology services include:

- An evaluation of the child's need for assistive technology
- Training for the child, family members, and educators about how to use an assistive technology device
- Instruction in how to operate or use a device
- Modifying or customizing a device
- Training school personnel to use the device to ensure that the device is used appropriately

My child has a severe hearing impairment. He needs an FM system. The school does not agree. What now?

The law requires IEP teams to "consider the communication needs of the child, and in the case of a child who is deaf or hard of hearing, consider the child's language and communication needs, opportunities for direct communication with peers and professional personnel in the child's language and communication mode, academic level, and full range of needs."

The team must also "consider whether the child requires assistive technology devices and services."[4]

Write a letter to the IEP team. Include a brief description of your child's disability. Request an IEP meeting to review your child's communication needs and his need for assistive listening technology, specifically an FM system.

If your child sees an audiologist in private practice, ask the audiologist to write a strong letter about the child's need for the FM system, and the impact on his education if the school refuses to provide the FM system.

Evaluating Assistive Technology Products

- Where will the A.T. device or tool be used (e.g., home, school, work and/or social settings)? If the A.T. device will be used in more than one setting, is it portable?
- How easy is it to learn to use?
- Is it reliable?
- Is it compatible with other technologies?
- Is technical support available? Does the manufacturer offer online help or a toll-free number?
- What is the quality of the visual display and/or auditory output (if applicable)?

TIP: Try before you buy an A.T. device.

Source: Consumer Tips for Evaluating Assistive Technology Products by Marshall Raskind, Ph.D.

www.greatschools.net/LD/assistive-technology/evaluating-consumer-AT-products.gs?content=783

A.T. Evaluations and Plans

My child needs assistive technology. Can I request this evaluation?

Yes. Ask the IEP team to refer your child for an evaluation by an assistive technology specialist. The specialist will evaluate your child and identify her needs. An assistive technology evaluation may include a functional evaluation of the child in school or at home.

If the IEP team agrees to your request for an assistive technology evaluation, they should include the assessment in the IEP.

The expected date to start and finish the assistive technology evaluation should also be in the IEP.

Assistive technology specialists have special knowledge and expertise. If your child's needs are complex or you anticipate resistance, ask the assistive technology specialist to join the IEP team.

Some of my students with IEPs need assistive technology. When should the IEP team provide a technology device or service?

Assistive technology is likely to be appropriate when it does one or more of the following:

- Allows a child to perform functions that cannot be achieved by other means
- Enables a child to approximate normal fluency or rate, or a level of accomplishment that cannot be achieved by other means
- Allows a child to participate in programs or activities that otherwise would be closed to the child
- Increases the child's endurance or ability to complete tasks that are too laborious to be attempted on a routine basis
- Allows the child to concentrate on learning, not mechanical tasks
- Provides greater access to the general curriculum
- Supports normal social interactions with peers and adults
- Allows the child to participate in the least restrictive educational environment

The IEP team agreed that my child needs a laptop to do classwork. The school provides a laptop at school. He needs the laptop to do homework assignments. Can he bring the laptop home?

Probably. The IEP team decides if your child needs an assistive technology device at home or in other places. Does the team know your child needs to use the laptop at home to receive a free, appropriate public education? If the team agrees that he needs to use the laptop at home, this must be included in his IEP.[5]

Recommended Resources

Assistive Technology Checklist from the Wisconsin Assistive Technology Initiative

www.atp.ne.gov/techassist.ATcklist-WATI.pdf

Isn't assistive technology intended for students with severe physical disabilities?

Assistive technologies are simply devices that help people compensate for deficits, regardless of severity.

Eyeglasses are an A.T. device. Children with learning disabilities who have deficits in reading or writing benefit from the word processing and voice recognition capabilities of computers, text-to-speech and word prediction software to help them access the general curriculum (e.g., social studies, science, geography).

"For people without disabilities, technology makes things easier. For people with disabilities, technology makes things possible."

- Dr. Katherine Seelman

If a child has severe mental or physical disabilities, assistive technology can help the child with more complex problems.

Some of my students with IEPs use calculators. They do not learn how to solve math problems because they depend on the calculator – isn't the calculator a crutch?

Assistive technology is not a substitute for teaching children skills like reading and math. Assistive technology should help children learn skills and perform tasks. With assistive technology, children can learn and interact with teachers and peers.

If the assistive technology is appropriate, it helps the child compensate and function more normally.

If a child needs assistive technology to have access to the general curriculum and benefit from education, it is not a crutch. Although a child may depend on a device to perform, not allowing a child to use the device will prevent the child from learning and receiving an appropriate education.

Assume you need glasses to read this book. Should you be forbidden from using glasses to read?

As a regular education teacher, you need to discuss your concerns that your students are not learning to solve math problems with their parents and their IEP teams.

My child has an A.T. device written into her IEP. The teacher doesn't know how to use the device so it isn't used. How can we make sure teachers are trained to use A.T. devices?

If your child's IEP says she will have assistive technology, the school must provide it.

The law requires schools to provide assistive technology services, including training for the teachers, child, and family.[6] Your child's teachers may need training so they know how to use a device. Your child and your family may need A.T. services so you can learn to use a device. Assistive technology services, **including training**, need to be written in the child's IEP.

Your school district may have staff members who are qualified to provide training. Parent Training and Information Centers, State Tech Act programs, and A.T. vendors also provide training.

TIP: If your child changes teachers during the year or a new teacher is hired, the school needs to ensure that the new teacher is appropriately trained on how to use the A.T. device.

Choosing to use the device is not optional for a teacher. After the teacher is trained, a follow-up should be scheduled to observe the student and teacher using the device.

Strategies for Assistive Technology Negotiations

If you are negotiating for A.T., Dr. Dave Edyburn helps you respond to statements like this:

- We determined that your child will not benefit from assistive technology ...
- We don't want your child to become dependent on a text-reader ...
- Your child is not the only child who struggles with this problem ...
- We will provide some technology but there is no need to write it in the IEP ...
- We can't afford that ...

www.adcadvocacy.net/ATNegotiationsStrategies20408.htm

Universal Design for Learning

What is Universal Design for Learning (UDL)?

Universal design for learning (UDL) is a set of principles for designing curriculum that provides all individuals with equal opportunities to learn. Grounded in research of learner differences and effective instructional settings, UDL principles call for varied and flexible ways to:

- Present or access information, concepts, and ideas (the "what" of learning),
- Plan and execute learning tasks (the "how" of learning)
- Get engaged - and stay engaged - in learning

How can UDL help my child?

Children come to school with a variety of skills, abilities, needs, interests, backgrounds, and learning styles. This diversity is confirmed by neuroscience. Brain imaging technologies show the different ways learners respond to educational tasks and environments.

Often curriculum – which includes the goals, methods, assessments, and materials we use to teach and learn – is fixed and inflexible. This turns individual differences into barriers as learners try to bend their individual styles, skills, and abilities to the curriculum's needs.

Print textbooks are the most common technology in classrooms. Many children with disabilities need textbooks in different formats. Struggling students can gain access to the general curriculum by using materials that allow them to:

Hear text spoken aloud

See text displayed in custom colors

In different fonts,

In larger sizes

Or any of these combinations

Recommended Resources

Glossary of Assistive Technology Terms from the Family Center on Technology and Disability

www.fctd.info/show/glossary

The National Instructional Materials Accessibility Standard (NIMAS) creates a national standard for print materials in accessible formats.[7] Schools and publishers must adhere to these standards when creating educational materials – textbooks, workbooks, and supplemental materials. NIMAS also requires states to provide instructional materials in a timely manner.

Your child's IEP team determines your child's need for materials in an alternate format. The team must document the child's needs and required supports in the child's IEP.[8] IEP teams need to be familiar with UDL and NIMAS.

In Summation

In this chapter you learned about assistive technology devices and services and when you should request an assistive technology evaluation.

You learned that IEP teams must consider each child's needs for assistive technology. The law requires all decisions about assistive technology devices and services to be individualized.

You also learned about Universal Design for Learning and how UDL can help children learn.

In the next chapter you will learn about transition planning and transition services. Transition services must be individualized to meet your child's unique needs. The goal of transition is to prepare your child for a successful transition to life after school.

You will also learn about self-advocacy skills that your child must learn.

Endnotes

1. 20 U.S.C. § 1414(d)(3)(B)(v)
2. 20 U.S.C. § 1400(c)(5)(H)
3. 20 U.S.C. § 1401(1)
4. 34 C.F.R. § 1414(d)(3)(A)(iv) and (v)
5. 20 U.S.C. § 1412(a)(1); 20 U.S.C. § 1412 (a)(12)(B)(i); 34 C.F.R. § 300.105
6. 20 U.S.C. § 1401(2)
7. 20 U.S.C. § 1412(23)
8. ***Building the Legacy, Module 8*** www.nichyc.org/laws/idea/pages/buildingthelegacy.aspx

9 Transition to Life After School

- Transition Assessments
- Transition Services
- Transition Plans with Measurable Goals
- Transfer of Rights at Age of Majority
- Graduation from High School
- Self-Advocacy Skills

In this chapter, you will learn about transition plans and services. You will learn about using transition assessments to create measurable transition goals.[1] You will also learn about the transfer of rights at the age of majority and graduation from high school.

As a parent, you play an important role in transition planning. You contribute information to transition assessments.

You encourage your child to think about her strengths, interests, and preferences. You help other IEP team members identify measurable goals that your child wants to achieve. You are more likely to "think out of the box" in looking for solutions to help your child.

Transition Assessments

What are transition assessments?

Transition assessments allow you and other members of the IEP team to identify your child's unique needs, preferences, interests, and strengths. Transition assessments are formal and informal.

Formal assessments are standardized tests that have data showing that they are reliable and valid.

Informal transition assessments are subjective. Examples of informal assessments are paper/pencil tests, observations, interviews, and functional skill inventories.

Transition experts recommend that IEP teams use a variety of evaluations.[2]

Transition Assessments include:

- adaptive behavior assessments
- general and specific aptitude tests
- interest and work values inventories
- intelligence tests
- achievement tests
- personality and preference tests
- career maturity or readiness tests
- self-determination assessments
- work-related temperament scales
- transition planning inventories

"Age Appropriate Transition Guide," National Secondary Transition Technical Assistance Center at www.nsttac.org/pdf/transition_guide/nsttac_tag.pdf

Transition Services

Special education for children with disabilities is "designed to meet their unique needs and prepare them for further education, employment, and independent living."[3]

Transition services must be included in the first IEP that is in effect when your child turns 16 (in most cases, this is the IEP developed when he is 15). Transition services may be included in the IEPs of younger children if the IEP team decides this is appropriate.[4] Some states have a lower age for transition services.

What are transition services?

Transition services prepare your child for life after school. Transition services:

- Improve your child's academic and functional achievement
- Are individualized, based on your child's needs, and take into account his strengths, preferences, and interests
- Include instruction, related services, community experiences, employment, and adult living skills
- Include daily living skills and a functional vocational evaluation[5]

My 15 year-old needs help with transition planning. When will he be eligible for transition services?

Transition planning is an essential part of a child's special education program. Appropriate transition services will help your child make a successful transition to life after high school.[6]

Since transition services must be included in the first IEP in effect when your child turns 16, when he is 15, write a letter to request an IEP meeting to discuss your child's transition needs, goals, and the services he will need to meet these goals.

Transition Services include:

- College and continuing education
- Vocational education
- Integrated and supported employment
- Independent living and community participation
- Courses of study and advanced placement courses to prepare for future education

Is my child a member of the IEP team?

Yes! We encourage parents to invite their children to IEP meetings as soon as they believe it is appropriate. If your child does not attend the IEP meeting, the team must take steps to determine his strengths, preferences, and interests.

If the IEP team will discuss your child's transition services and/or postsecondary goals, the team **must** invite your child to the meeting. The team must also invite you and notify you of the purpose of the meeting.[7]

My 15 year-old has cognitive impairments and cerebral palsy. He functions below his peer group. Does the IEP team have to develop measurable transition goals, regardless of my child's skill levels?

Yes. The first IEP in effect when your child turns 16, or younger if the IEP team agrees this is appropriate, must include measurable transition goals based on transition assessments. This applies to all IEPs for all children with disabilities who will be 16 years old.

Your child's unique needs are determined by age-appropriate transition assessments in several areas (training, education, employment, and independent living skills). The measurable transition goals must meet your child's unique needs.[8]

Can the IEP Team decide to address transition before age 16 (for example, at age 14)?

Yes. The IEP team can decide to develop a transition plan for a child who is younger than age 15 or 16. Any transition plan must include measurable goals and the transition services needed to meet these goals.

My child is 14 years old. When I requested transition services and a transition plan, the IEP team said they don't have to provide transition services until he is 16. Is this correct?

Nope! Transition services **must be included** in the IEP that is in effect when your child turns 16 (in general, that IEP will be developed when he is 15). The team can plan for transition long before your child is 16 if they decide this is appropriate.

Write a letter requesting an IEP meeting to discuss your child's unique needs related to his disability and his transition needs. You need to make your case about why transition planning should begin early. Do research on transition for children with his disability. Bring extra copies of documents for the IEP team members to support your position.

Transition Plans with Measurable Goals

The IEP team must develop appropriate measurable transition goals for the transition plan. These goals are included in your child's IEPs. The goals must be based on "age appropriate transition assessments related to training, education, employment, and, where appropriate, independent living skills."[9]

How does the IEP team determine measurable transition goals for my child?

The IEP team will use transition assessments to develop measurable transition goals. After the team decides on measurable transition goals, the school is required to provide the transition services your child needs to meet these goals.

My tenth-grader has been in special ed since 3rd grade. He has learning disabilities. He is depressed and wants to drop out of school. I'm terrified about his future. Can transition planning help?

Maybe. Twice as many children with disabilities drop out of school, when compared to students who are not disabled.[10] Of students who drop out, 36% have learning disabilities and 59% have emotional and/or behavioral disabilities.[11]

One purpose of transition planning and services is to reduce the number of children with disabilities who drop out of school. To be effective, the transition plan must be individualized and implemented properly. The IEP team must work closely with you and your child to implement the plan.

Transition plans can include academic and non-academic courses, employment, and training opportunities. If the team selects courses of study that are meaningful to your child, this may increase his motivation to stay in school.[12]

Transition should help your child understand his disability and what he needs to be successful. Transition can include decisions about where to live and what to do for fun.

Advocate's TIP

Begin Transition Planning Early

Transition planning should include services from other agencies –for example, a 504 Plan for college or a referral to Vocational Rehabilitation. Parents need to get service providers involved in transition planning early.

- Dan Cavallini, Ed.D., Special Education Tutor, Career and Technology Magnet

At the last IEP meeting, the team decided that Vocational Rehabilitation would evaluate my child and provide transition services, including job training. Several months passed with no evaluation and no job training. The school says this is not their responsibility.

This is the school's responsibility. The school is required to provide your child with a free, appropriate public education. The IEP team decided that your child needed a transition evaluation and job training. The team selected Vocational Rehabilitation to provide these services.

If an agency drops the ball and does not provide the services in the IEP, the IEP team is responsible for finding another way to provide these services. The team may identify other providers or agencies to provide services in the IEP.[13]

IEP team members need to keep the lines of communication between school, home, and other agencies open. If services will be provided by another agency, the odds of problems increase.

Transfer of Rights at Age of Majority

The Individuals with Disabilities Education Act (IDEA) authorizes the transfer of educational decision-making rights from the parent to the child at the age of majority.

What is "age of majority?"

Age of majority is the legal age under your state law when an individual becomes an adult. In most states, the age of majority is 18, but there are exceptions. Be sure to check your state special education regulations to find the age of majority in your state.

What happens in a transfer of rights?

Educational rights transfer to the student when she reaches the age of majority. Educational rights include the right to:

- Receive notice of and attend Individual Education Program (IEP) meetings
- Consent to a reevaluation
- Consent to a change in placement
- Request mediation or a due process hearing to resolve a dispute about issues related to providing a free appropriate public education (FAPE)

How will I know if or when educational rights transfer to my child?

The school must provide you and your child with notice that your parental rights will transfer to your child when she reaches the age of majority. No later than one year before your child reaches the age of majority, the IEP must include a statement that the child was informed that rights will transfer.[14]

My son is nearly 18 so his educational rights will transfer soon. Without my input, I'm afraid he'll drop out or accept a diploma that will end his eligibility for special education and related services. What can I do to prevent this from happening?

You are right to be concerned. Transferring legal rights to young adults who are unable to make informed decisions is risky. This allows young adults to make decisions that may affect the quality of their lives forever.[15] Several legal cases involve a school "graduating" a child who was clearly not prepared, without the parent's knowledge or consent.

If possible, have your child write a statement that says, "I [child's name], pursuant to 20 U.S.C. 1415(m) and [your state's special education regulation section], hereby appoint my parent, [your name], to represent my educational interests." If your child is able, have this statement written in longhand, signed, and dated. Use the language in your state's special education regulation verbatim if you can. If possible, do not paraphrase it.

You can also obtain a "grant of authority" or educational "power of attorney" so you can continue to represent your child's educational interests. Consult with an attorney who is licensed to practice in your state for information about the best way to proceed.

Graduation from High School

Notice Before Graduation

Graduation is a change in placement so the school must notify you before they propose to graduate your child. This notice is intended to allow you and your child time to plan for (or challenge) graduation. Notice must be given a reasonable time before graduation.

My child graduated from high school with a regular diploma. Is she still eligible for services from the public school?

No. When your child graduates from high school with a regular diploma, her eligibility for special education ends.

My 19 year-old earned a GED. Now he is having second thoughts. Is he still eligible for special education services?

Maybe. If your child received a General Educational Diploma (GED), IEP diploma, or certificate of attendance, and the school did not evaluate him, he should still be eligible for special education services. His eligibility ends when he graduates high school with a regular diploma or he "ages out" of special education.[16]

Advocate's TIP

When a Diploma Isn't a Real Diploma

You need to understand the diploma options in your school district. One state offers an "Occupational Diploma." Most parents assume that an occupational diploma is a regular high school diploma. These parents are shocked when they learn that their child who received an occupational diploma is not eligible to attend a technical school or community college.

- Susan Bruce, Regional Education Coordinator, PRO*Parents of South Carolina, Inc

Summary of Performance

My child will soon graduate from high school. We received a document called

"Summary of Academic Achievement and Functional Performance." What is this?

When your child graduates from high school with a regular diploma or "ages out" of special education, the school must provide her with a "summary of academic achievement and functional performance."

The information in the Summary of Performance is based on your child's unique needs and her goals after she graduates from high school. The Summary should include recommendations about ways to help meet her [post-secondary] goals.[17]

My son just got a GED. Will he receive a Summary of Performance?

Probably not. The law requires schools to provide a Summary of Performance to children who will not be eligible for special education services after they graduate from high school with a regular diploma, or "age out." If your son was eligible for special education when he earned the GED, he may still be eligible.[18]

If a child leaves school without a regular high school diploma, such as a GED or alternate diploma, the child's eligibility for special education does not end.[19]

Is the school required to provide documentation to determine a student's eligibility for Vocational Rehabilitation services?

No. The law does not require schools to provide the documentation to determine if a student is eligible for another program or service, like Vocational Rehabilitation. However, the Summary of Performance should include information that will help another program determine if the student is eligible for their services.[20]

Is the school required to provide documentation that will allow my child to receive accommodations in college or another educational program?

No. If your child will need accommodations from a college or university, the Summary of Performance may be part of the documentation used by the college to determine if she qualifies for accommodations.

You may want to request a reevaluation during the last year of high school to establish your child's eligibility for special education. Some colleges will provide 504 accommodations if the student was eligible in high school and the testing is less than three years old.

Self-Advocacy Skills

Self-advocacy is the ability to understand and effectively communicate your needs to others. Learning to be an effective self-advocate is all about educating the people around you. Knowledge is the key to self-advocacy. Like anything else, the more you know, the better you understand, and the easier it is to explain.[21]

This journey of self-education is an ongoing process, as your needs change over time. There are three parts to becoming an effective self-advocate: know yourself, know your needs, and know how to get what you need.

Know Yourself

Diagnostic testing is the first step towards understanding your needs. A psycho-educational evaluation is a series of tests used to diagnose disabilities and to identify individual strengths and weaknesses.

The results and recommendations should be clearly stated in a written report, and clearly explained in a meeting with the evaluator. You should know your skills levels, strengths, and weaknesses.

Know What You Need

You need to know your skills, strengths, and weaknesses. Learn about your disability and how it affects your daily activities, communications, and social interactions.

Accommodations compensate for disabilities, and vary from person to person based on the type of disability and the degree to which it interferes with daily activities.

Communication takes practice and can be emotionally draining. It's easy to get caught-up in feelings of guilt that you are asking for "special treatment," or that you don't need an accommodation because you excel in other areas. Having a supportive friend and/or support group to help "coach" you through this process is important to keeping you grounded.

Know How to Get What You Need

The Americans with Disabilities Act Amendments Act (ADAAA) requires public and private institutions to provide "reasonable accommodations" to individuals with a documented disability. Employers and universities are prohibited from discriminating against a person with a disability if they are "otherwise qualified."

Documenting communications and interactions in a journal and keeping copies of all letters, e-mails, policies, and procedures is a good way to provide information if you have difficulty getting your accommodations and you need to file a complaint.

Understanding your rights and knowing how to clearly communicate with others in a constructive way is just as important as clearly communicating your disability and individual needs.

The better you understand your disability, needs, and rights, and the better you can communicate and document this information, the easier self-advocacy will become.

Self-education, effective communication, and maintaining a support system are your keys to becoming an effective self-advocate.

Transition Checklist

Your child's transition plan must be based on age-appropriate transition assessments. The transition plan must include measurable goals that are updated annually. The plan also must include transition services to enable the child to meet the transition goals.

1. Does the transition plan include appropriate measurable postsecondary goals that focus on education, training, employment, and independent living if needed?
Can the goal(s) be counted? Will the goal(s) occur after the student graduates from school?
Based on information about the student, are the transition goals appropriate? Y N

2. Are the postsecondary goals updated annually when the current IEP was developed?
Y N

3. Does the IEP or the child's file include evidence that the measurable goals are based on age appropriate transition assessments? Y N

4. Is it likely that the transition services in the IEP will enable the child to meet his postsecondary goals?
Is the transition plan based on a functional vocational evaluation, with services to meet the transition goals? Y N

5. Does the transition plan include courses of study that align with the student's transition goals? Y N

6. Does the IEP include measurable transition goals related to the student's transition services needs? Y N

7. Is there evidence in the IEP or in the file that the student was invited to attend the IEP meeting where transition services were discussed? Y N

8. Does the IEP include evidence that a representative of a participating agency was invited to the IEP meeting? Y N NA

a. Was consent obtained from the parent (or the student at the age of majority)? Y N
b. If a participating agency is likely to be responsible for providing or paying for transition services, but no invitation is found, circle N.
c. If it is too soon to determine if the child will be involved with an outside agency, or no agency is likely to provide or pay for transition services, circle NA
d. If consent from the parent or student was not obtained, circle NA.

Does the transition plan comply with the legal requirements for transition plans? Y N

(If questions 1-8 were answered "yes," the IEP met the legal requirements for transition plans. If any questions were answered "no," the IEP did not meet the legal requirements for transition plans.)

This Transition Checklist is from the National Secondary Transition Technical Assistance Center. For more information, go to www.nsttac.org/pdf/checklista.pdf

In Summation

In this chapter you learned about transition plans, assessments, and measurable transition goals. You learned that the IEP team must develop measurable transition goals, and that goals must be based on transition assessments.

You also learned about the transfer of rights to your child at the age of majority, and new issues that arise when your child graduates from high school, with or without a regular high school diploma.

In the next chapter you will learn about the least restrictive environment and placement decisions.

Endnotes

1. 20 U.S.C. § 1414(d)(1)(A)(i)(VIII)
2. *Age Appropriate Transition Assessment Guide* from the National Center on Secondary Education and Transition (NCSET). www.nsttac.org/pdf/transition_guide/nsttac_tag.pdf
3. 20 U.S.C. § 1400(d)
4. 20 U.S.C. § 1414(d)(1)(A)(i)(VIII); 34 C.F.R. § 300.322(b)(2)
5. 20 U.S.C.§ 1401(34); 34 C.F.R. § 300.43
6. H. Rep. No. 105-95, pp. 101-102 (1997); S. Rep. No. 105-17, p. 22 (1997); Appendix A, Question #11
7. 34 C.F.R. § 300.321(b)(1)
8. 34 C.F.R. § 300.320(b)
9. 20 U.S.C. 1414(d)(1)(A)(i)(VIII)(aa)
10. H. Rep. No. 105-95, p. 85 (1997), S. Rep. No. 105-17, p. 5 (1997)
11. Blackorby, J., & Wagner, M. (1996). "Longitudinal post-school outcomes of youth with disabilities: Findings from the National Longitudinal Transition Study." *Exceptional Children*, 62(5), 399-413
12. Appendix A, Question #11
13. 20 U.S.C. § 1414(d)(6); 34 C.F.R. § 300.324(c)
14. 20 U.S.C. § 1415(m); 34 C.F.R. § 300.320(c)
15. *Age of Majority: Preparing Your Child for Making Good Choices* from the National Center on Secondary Education and Transition. www.ncset.org/publications/viewdesc.asp?id=318
16. 20 U.S.C. § 1414(c)(5)(B)
17. 34 C.F.R. § 300.305(e)(3). See a Sample Summary at www.docstoc.com/docs/2299958/Summary-of-Academic-Achievement
18. 20 U.S.C. § 1414 (c)(5); 34 C.F.R. § 300.305(e)(3)
19. 34 C.F.R. § 300.102(a)(3)(iv)
20. *OSEP Q and A on Secondary Transition: Building the Legacy: IDEA 2004* http://idea.ed.gov/explore/view/p/%2Croot%2Cdynamic%2CQaCorner%2C10%2C
21. The section about self advocacy is from *Self Advocacy: Know Yourself, What You Need and How to Get It* by Nancy Suzanne James. www.wrightslaw.com/info/sec504.selfadvo.ld.johnson.htm

10 Placement

- Placement Decisions
- Continuum of Alternative Placements
- Least Restrictive Environment (LRE)
- Children Placed in Private Schools

In this chapter, you will learn about special education placements — who makes placement decisions and what factors they must consider.

You will also learn about the requirements to place children with disabilities in the "least restrictive environment" and to provide a "continuum of alternative placements." You will learn the rules that govern special education for children who are placed in private schools.

Disagreements between parents and schools about placement are not unusual. Some school districts develop one-size-fits-all programs for children with disabilities and do not offer a continuum of alternative placements.

This practice runs counter to the legal requirements for individualized decisions about special education programs and placements in the least restrictive environment, with supplementary aids and services.

The Individuals with Disabilities Education Act (IDEA) says that special education is "a service for children rather than a place where such children are sent."[1]

When you think about placement decisions, keep that concept in mind.

Placement Decisions

After the IEP team makes decisions about your child's needs and the special education program, a team will decide your child's placement — where the services will be provided. Placement decisions must be individualized and based on your child's unique needs as described in the IEP.[2]

Who decides where my child will be placed?

In some states, the IEP team makes the placement decision. In other states, the decision may be made by another group of people who are knowledgeable about the child.

Do I have a say in decisions about my child's placement?

Yes. Parents are members of any group that decides their child's educational placement.[3] The team must include people who know:

- The child
- What the evaluation results mean
- What types of placements are appropriate

How does the team decide on a child's placement?

The first option the team must consider is placement in the general education classroom at the school your child would attend if not disabled.[4] The team needs to answer these questions:

- Can this child be educated satisfactorily in the general education classroom?
- What supplementary aids, services, and supports does the child need to be educated in the general education classroom?[5]

Are there any rules about placement decisions?

Yes. Your child's placement must be:

- Based on your child's unique needs as documented in the IEP
- Determined at least once a year
- As close to your child's home as possible so your child can be educated in the school he would attend if he was not disabled.[6]

Your child's placement may **not** be based on:

- Your child's disability category or label or severity of the disability (i.e., children with autism are placed in a class with other children with autism)

- The school's service delivery model (i.e., all children with learning disabilities receive "pull" or resource services)
- The availability of special education and related services, staff location, or school district convenience.[7]

Continuum of Alternative Placements

The Individuals with Disabilities Education Act requires that schools provide a continuum of alternative placements for children with disabilities.[8]

What is the "continuum of alternative placements?"

The continuum of alternative placements refers to places where children receive special education services. Placements are on a continuum, from least to most restrictive. Your child's placement may be in:

- A regular class, with needed supplementary aids and services
- A special class where all children receive special education services for some or most of the day
- A special school
- Home
- A hospital or other institution
- Another setting

In making a placement decision, the team must look at the full continuum of placement options.[9]

What is the relationship between placement decisions and supplementary aids, services, and supports?

Supplementary aids and services allow children with disabilities to be educated in regular education classes. Supplementary aids and services include direct services and supports for your child, and training for teachers and others who will work with your child. Examples of supplementary aids and services are:

- Modifications to the regular education curriculum
- Assistance from a teacher with special education training
- Special education training for the regular education teacher[10]

But that's not all. The IEP must also include a "statement of the specific special education and related services to be provided . . . and the extent that the child will be able to participate in regular education programs."

The team must look at your child's unique educational needs before deciding on the related services and supplementary aids and services she needs. See Chapter 5 to learn more about related services and supplementary aids and services.

Least Restrictive Environment (LRE)

The IEP team talked about placing my daughter in the "least restrictive environment." What does that mean?

The law requires schools to educate children with disabilities in regular education classes with children who are not disabled "to the maximum extent possible."[11]

Your child may not be removed from regular education classes unless the nature or severity of the disability does not allow her to be educated in regular classes, even with supplementary aids and services.[12]

If the team decides that your child can be educated in regular education classes if she receives appropriate supplementary aids and services, this is the least restrictive environment for your child.

My 6th grader has learning disabilities. He has received special education services in a resource class for four years but is still reading at the 2nd to 3rd grade level. I asked for one-on-one tutoring. The team said he must be educated in the regular classroom, with special ed services from an aide. Is this correct?

The law does not require every student to be placed in the regular classroom, regardless of the child's abilities and needs. If a child does not learn in the regular education classroom, this is not an appropriate placement for that child.

Your child needs to be taught by a highly qualified teacher, not an aide.

The law requires schools to make available a range or continuum of placement options to meet your child's unique educational needs. The school must offer the alternative placements listed in the definition of special education:

- Regular classes
- Special classes
- Special schools
- Home instruction
- Instruction in hospitals and institutions[13]

My child's school is an "inclusion school." What does that mean?

The term "inclusion" is not in the law. In general, when people talk about inclusion, they are referring to the "least restrictive environment" (LRE).

LRE means that schools must educate children with disabilities in regular classrooms with nondisabled children unless your child's individual needs require a different plan.

Placing children in special classes, separate schools or removing children from the regular education environment may occur if the nature or severity of the disability does not allow the child to be educated in regular classes.

My child is verbal and high functioning. The team placed her in a self-contained class of non-verbal boys with behavior problems. She needs to be in regular classes with other children her age. Any advice?

In deciding a child's placement, the team must consider any potential harmful effect on the child and the quality of services she needs.[14]

Write a letter to request a meeting to review and revise your child's IEP. Describe your child and her needs. Explain why you believe the current placement is harmful and will damage her.

If your daughter has been evaluated by or received treatment from a medical or mental health professional in the private sector, ask the professional to write a letter about your daughter, her strengths, weaknesses, needs, and the impact this placement will have on her. Ask the expert to describe an appropriate program and placement that will provide a free, appropriate public education in the least restrictive environment.

Our son attends the regional school for children who are blind and have other visual impairments. He is doing well and meeting his IEP goals. The school sent a letter saying they have to place him in the "nearest school" to our home because of the "least restrictive environment" requirement. Does the "least restrictive environment" always mean the "nearest" school?

No. A child's placement is not always at the "nearest" school. The law does not intend for schools to use a one-size-fits-all approach to educating all children with disabilities.

Placement decisions must be individualized and based on your child's unique needs. An appropriate placement in the least restrictive environment for one child may not be the same for another child with the same disability.

Your child is blind and attends school with other children who are visually impaired. To remove him from a placement where he is doing well is likely to damage him. This is not what the law intends. Write a letter to request a meeting with the IEP team. Describe your son's situation and your objections to changing his placement. Ask the team to reconsider their decision.

The IEP team plans to change our child's placement over our objections. What can we do?

Write a letter that describes your child's needs and why you object to this proposed change.

If the team proposes to change your child's identification, evaluation, or placement, they must provide you with written notice of the proposed change.

The law includes specific requirements for the prior written notice. It must:

- Describe the action proposed or refused by the school

- Explain why the school proposes or refuses to take the action
- Describe each evaluation procedure, assessment, record, or report that the school used as a basis for the proposed or refused action
- Include a statement that the parents of the child are protected under the procedural safeguards section of the law
- Provide sources for parents to contact for assistance in understanding these provisions
- Describe the other options the IEP team considered and the reasons why these options were rejected
- Describe the factors relevant to the school's proposal or refusal

This safeguard about prior written notice also applies if you request a change and the school refuses to make that change.[15]

Children Placed in Private Schools

The public school wants to place our child in a private school. If we agree, who is responsible for developing his IEP?

Before the school can place your child in a private school, the district must hold a meeting to develop an IEP for your child. The district must ensure that a representative of the private school attends this meeting. If a representative of the private school cannot attend the meeting, the school must use other methods to ensure that the private school participates in the meeting (i.e., individual or conference calls).[16]

If your child is placed in a private school, the public school must decide whether to allow the private school to review and revise your child's IEP. The public school must ensure that you and a representative of the public school are involved in all decisions about your child's IEP.

Who is responsible for ensuring that an IEP is implemented in a private school?

Your school district is responsible for providing your child with a free, appropriate public education (FAPE), so the district is responsible for ensuring that the private school implements the IEP. If the private school implements the IEP, the responsibility for compliance remains with the school district and the state department of education (SEA).

If the district places your child in a private school, your child has all the rights of a child with a disability who attends a public school.

Your state department of education (SEA) must ensure that your child continues to receive the special education and related services in her IEP at no cost to you. The state department of education also must ensure that your child receives an education that meets state and local standards.

In Summation

In this chapter you learned how a team makes placement decisions and what criteria they must use. You learned that the school must offer a continuum of alternate placements. Your child's placement should be in the least restrictive environment. The IEP team must consider the regular education classroom as the first placement option.

You learned that if the school refuses to change your child's placement, they must provide you with "prior written notice" with detailed information about their refusal.

If the district places your child in a private school setting, the district is responsible for ensuring that your child continues to receive a free, appropriate public education.

In the next chapter you will learn about reviewing and revising the IEP.

Endnotes

1. 20 U.S.C. § 1400(c)(5)(C)
2. Commentary in 71 FR at 46588
3. 20 U.S.C. § 1414(e); 34 C.F.R. § 300.327; also ***Guide to the IEP: Deciding Placements*** from the U.S. Department of Education. www.ed.gov/parents/needs/speced/iepguide/index.html#deciding
4. 34 C.F.R. § 300.116
5. 34 C.F.R. § 300.42; 34 C.F.R. § 300.114 - 300.116
6. 20 U.S.C. § 1412(a)(5); 34 C.F.R § 300.314 - 300.317
7. Commentary in 71 FR at 46588
8. 20 U.S.C. § 1412(a)(5); 34 C.F.R. § 300.115
9. 34 C.F.R. § 300.115
10. ***Questions and Answers on Least Restrictive Environment (LRE) Requirements of the IDEA*** published by the U.S. Department of Education, Office of Special Education and Rehabilitative Services. www.wrightslaw.com/info/lre.osers.memo.idea.htm
11. 34 C.F.R. § 300.114(a)(2)
12. 34 C.F.R. § 300.114(a)(2)
13. 20 U.S.C. § 1412(a)(5); 34 C.F.R. § 300.115
14. 34 C.F.R. § 300.116(d)
15. 20 U.S.C. § 1415(c)(1); 34 C.F.R § 300.503
16. 34 C.F.R. § 300.325

11 Reviewing and Revising the IEP

- When to Review and Revise an IEP
- Revising the IEP by Agreement
- Notifying School Staff of Changes in the IEP
- Timelines

In this chapter, you will learn about requesting a meeting to review and revise your child's IEP. You will learn about problems that should trigger a meeting to review and revise, and a new provision in the law that allows parents and schools to amend the IEP by agreement.

You will also learn about the school's requirements to notify school personnel about their new responsibilities after an IEP is revised.

When to Review and Revise an IEP

At least once a year, the school will schedule a meeting to review your child's IEP.[1] During this meeting, you and other IEP team members will review:

- Your child's strengths
- Results of recent evaluations
- Your child's academic, developmental, and functional needs
- Your concerns about enhancing your child's education

After reviewing this information, the team will develop an IEP for the next academic year or sooner.

Who can request that an IEP be reviewed and revised?

A parent, teacher, or related services provider may decide that a child's IEP needs to be reviewed and revised early, before the annual review. The child may not be making sufficient progress to meet the IEP goals by the end of the academic year. He may be struggling in the general education environment. He may have mastered all the goals in his IEP and need new goals.

When can I request that my child's IEP be revised?

You can request that your child's IEP be reviewed or revised at any time. Here are a few problems that should trigger an IEP meeting to review and revise a child's IEP.

- Any lack of expected progress toward the annual goals and in the general education curriculum
- Information from any new evaluation or reevaluation[2]
- Information or concerns shared by the parent or teacher[3]
- The child's anticipated needs
- Other matters

I want to request a meeting to review and revise my child's IEP. Should I make my request in writing?

Yes. Although the law does not require you to request a meeting in writing, you should always put important requests in writing. In the letter, describe your concerns and the reasons you are requesting the meeting.

When you write a letter, you increase the odds that a school staff member will follow up on your request promptly. If you make a verbal request, don't be surprised if the person forgets.

What happens when the IEP team reviews and revises an IEP?

The process of reviewing and revising a child's IEP is similar to developing the annual IEP. The IEP team should review your child's progress toward the goals in the IEP.

The team should also update your child's present levels of academic achievement and functional performance and her needs. The team should use updated information to develop, update, or revise the IEP goals. If your child has been evaluated recently, the team must consider this evaluation.

My child isn't making progress so I asked for a meeting to revise the IEP. The school said they can't change the IEP because I signed it. Can a school refuse to review and revise an IEP for this reason?

That's ridiculous! You have a right to request an IEP meeting to review and revise your child's IEP at any time.[4] If, for example, you believe your child is not making satisfactory progress, or if you have a new evaluation, or if your child has achieved the IEP goals, you can and should request another IEP meeting.[5]

My child has had a "speech IEP" since first grade. Now he is in middle school. He is failing three classes. Is he entitled to special education services in these areas where he needs help?

Before your child was found eligible for speech-language therapy several years ago, the school was required to complete a comprehensive psycho-educational evaluation. An eligibility team decided that he was a child with a disability who needed speech-language therapy. It is likely that your child's needs have changed since that evaluation or subsequent reevaluations.

If your child is failing, request a meeting to review and revise your child's IEP. Remember, you can request a meeting when:

- Your child is not making expected progress on the annual IEP goals or in the general education curriculum
- You have results from any evaluation or reevaluation
- You, as a parent, have information to provide
- Your child's anticipated needs change

You may need to request an evaluation or get an evaluation from an evaluator in the private sector to gather the information and recommendations you need.

Revising the IEP by Agreement

Our child takes a social skills class. He wants to take history and science as electives and we agree. The school says we must convene the IEP team to change these classes. Can't we do this without involving the entire IEP team?

Yes. The law allows parents and schools to amend the IEP by agreement. This provision gives you the flexibility to amend an IEP in writing without convening the full IEP team.[6]

We revised our child's IEP by agreement. Because the IEP changed as a result of that agreement, the school says we are not entitled to the annual IEP review. Is this correct?

No. The law requires the IEP team to review your child's IEP at least annually to determine if the annual goals were achieved and to develop an IEP for next year. The option to amend the IEP by agreement does not replace the annual meeting to review and revise your child's IEP.[7]

If my child's IEP is reviewed and revised, does the entire IEP team have to attend the meeting?

No. If you and the school agree to amend or modify the IEP, you may revise the IEP by agreement without convening a meeting of the full IEP team. The group creates a written document that describes the changes or modifications in your child's IEP. The document should note that, by agreement of the parties, a full IEP meeting was not held.[8]

You should request and receive a copy of this revised IEP with the amendments.

The school wants to amend my child's IEP without a meeting. We do not feel comfortable with this plan. Can we ask for a team meeting instead?

Yes. You do not have to agree to amend the IEP without an IEP meeting.[9] Allowing parents and schools to revise the IEP without bringing the entire team together is convenient if small changes are being considered (i.e., adding or modifying an accommodation, changing a class schedule).

If significant changes may be made to your child's IEP (i.e., reducing or eliminating services or accommodations), it is usually not a good idea to revise the IEP by agreement.

In general, at least one of your child's regular education teachers should participate in a meeting to review and revise the IEP.[10] The team should also get input from the other teachers and related services providers.

The team must also consider the special factors described in Chapter 7. The team must examine if and/or how the special factor(s) are affecting her ability to learn and meet her IEP goals.[11] The team must also consider whether your child needs assistive technology.

Advocate's TIP

When modifying the IEP without an IEP meeting, make sure that the school representative who agrees to the changes is authorized to do so by the district.

- Candace Cortiella, The Advocacy Institute

Must our request to revise an IEP by agreement be in writing?

The law does not require that requests to revise an IEP by agreement be in writing. Despite this, we encourage parents to document their request, in writing. Since questions and misunderstandings about the agreement may crop up later, we recommend that both parties document the terms of the agreement.

The law does not require you to provide written consent to amend the IEP by agreement without a team meeting.[12] Any changes made to your child's IEP must be in writing.

Notifying School Staff of Changes in the IEP

We amended our child's IEP by agreement. We are worried that the teachers and service providers will not know about their new responsibilities. Will the school tell them about the changes in the IEP?

All your child's teachers and service providers must have access to the IEP. When your child's IEP is amended by agreement, the school is required to inform all members of the IEP team about the changes. This includes all teachers and related service providers.[13]

Despite this requirement, it's a good idea to be proactive and send a short note to the teachers and service providers to advise them that the IEP was revised. Include a copy of the revised IEP with changes highlighted.

Timelines

I wrote a letter to request a meeting to review and revise my child's IEP a month ago. The school has not responded. How long does the school have to schedule a meeting?

Good question. Federal law and federal special education regulations do not provide a time limit for reviewing and revising IEPs. This issue is left to the states to decide. You need to check your state special education regulations to see if your state created timelines to review and revise IEPs.

If your state does not provide a timeline, then the courts look at a standard of reasonableness. This standard may be just a few days, or longer, dependent upon the specific facts. A month is too long for inaction and no response. Hand deliver a nice follow up letter that restates your earlier request and include a copy of that earlier letter. The letter may have been lost or misplaced.

In Summation

In this chapter, you learned about reviewing and revising your child's IEP. You learned about problems that should trigger a meeting to review and revise the IEP, and a new provision in the law that allows parents and schools to amend the IEP by agreement.

In the next chapter, you will learn about Extended School Year (ESY) services, how ESY decisions are made, and by whom.

Endnotes

1. 20 U.S.C. § 1414(d)(4); 34 C.F.R. § 300.324 (b)
2. 34 C.F.R. § 300.303
3. 34 C.F.R. § 300.305(a)(2)
4. 121 Cong. Record, S20428-29 (Nov. 19, 1975)
5. Appendix A, Question #20
6. 34 C.F.R. § 300.324 (a)(6); Commentary in 71 FR at 46686
7. Commentary in 71 FR at 46685

8. 20 U.S.C. § 1414(d)(3)(D); 34 C.F.R. § 300.324(a)(4)
9. Commentary in 71 FR at 46685
10. 34 C.F.R. § 300.324(b)(3)
11. 34 C.F.R. § 300.324(b)(2)
12. Commentary in 71 FR at 46685
13. 34 C.F.R. § 300.323(d); 34 C.F.R. § 300.324(a)(4)(ii)

12 Extended School Year Services

- What are Extended School Year Services?
- Eligibility for ESY Services
- Factors to Consider
- How to Request ESY Services

In this chapter, you will learn about Extended School Year (ESY) services – what ESY services are, the purpose they serve, who makes eligibility decisions, and the criteria they must use.

You will learn that ESY services must be individualized to meet your child's needs.[1] You will also learn how ESY services differ from other summer school and summer remedial programs.

State departments of education establish the criteria for ESY services. Eligibility for ESY is influenced by legal decisions in state and federal courts. This leads to different eligibility criteria around the country.

You may receive incorrect information about ESY from school staff. For example, school

personnel may advise you that ESY services are not available for children in your child's disability category. Or, school staff may tell you that they only use "regression-recoupment" to determine if a child is eligible for ESY services.

Although these statements are legally incorrect, you need documentation to make your case.

Contact your state department of education. Ask for information they publish about Extended School Year services. Next, visit the web site of your state department of education. Search the site for information about "Extended School Year" and "ESY."

The information you receive will help you develop expertise about ESY services. Feel free to share this information with the staff at your child's school.

What are Extended School Year services?

Extended School Year (ESY) services are special education and related services for children with disabilities provided beyond the traditional academic year.

Some children with disabilities need ESY services to receive a free, appropriate public education (FAPE). If the child needs ESY services to receive a FAPE, the school is required to provide those services.

The child's IEP team decides if a child is eligible for ESY services. These decisions may be made at a regular IEP meeting or an ESY meeting. Services are based on the child's needs as described in the IEP.

The school may not limit ESY services to particular categories of disability, or unilaterally limit the type, amount, or duration of these services. The team must make decisions on a case-by-case basis. One child may need a full-day special education program during the summer. Another child may need related services, like speech-language therapy or physical therapy, two or three times a week. Another child may not be eligible for any ESY services.

Is ESY the same as summer school?

No. ESY services are different from summer school, summer remedial classes, and summer enrichment programs. ESY services are a continuation of your child's special education program as described in the IEP.

Can the school charge a fee for ESY services?

No. Because a child with a disability needs ESY services to receive a free, appropriate public education, schools cannot charge for these services.[4]

Are ESY services written into the IEP?

Yes. The IEP team should write all ESY services into your child's IEP. A separate IEP for ESY services is not necessary.

My district provides ESY for a few weeks when summer school is in session. My child needs more than a few weeks of ESY, but the school

says they don't have enough staff to provide more services.

Decisions about ESY services must be based on your child's needs, not on what's convenient for the school.

The school may not:

- Unilaterally limit the ESY services to a set number of days or hours of service[5]
- Allow ESY services to be limited by the financial resources of the school or restrict ESY services for administrative convenience

Should my child's placement for ESY services be in the least restrictive environment?

Yes. The requirements about placement in the least restrictive environment (LRE) apply to ESY services.

If a proposed ESY placement might isolate your child, the IEP team should consider whether an alternative is more appropriate. In some cases, the IEP team may determine that a more restrictive setting is necessary to provide your child with a free, appropriate public education.

The IEP team proposed that an aide provide my child's ESY program. Should a certified teacher provide these services?

Yes. Your child's teacher should be highly qualified. An aide is not qualified to teach children with disabilities.

TIP: Ask the teacher who provides ESY services to submit a report about your child's progress to the teacher(s) for the next school year, with a copy to you.

My child receives ESY services. Is the school responsible for transportation?

Yes. If your child's IEP includes ESY services, the school is responsible for ensuring that your child is transported to and from these services.

Eligibility for ESY Services

Who decides if my child will receive Extended School Year services?

Your child's IEP team decides if your child needs ESY services.[6] You are a member of that team.

My child has learning disabilities and has an IEP. He is in 6th grade but reads at the the 3rd grade level. When I asked for ESY services, the team said he is not eligible because they only provide ESY for children with severe disabilities. Is this correct?

No. The school may not limit ESY services to children in any predetermined disability category. The IEP team may not:

- Deny ESY services to children with disabilities who need these services to receive a free, appropriate public education (FAPE)

- Limit ESY services to predetermined disability categories
- Categorically exclude students with certain disabilities[7]

When I requested ESY services, the team said my child would not benefit from the program they offer. Can they make decisions based on what they have available?

No. The school may not offer a one-size-fits-all program of ESY services to all children with disabilities. The content of an ESY program must be individualized and based on the child's unique needs.[8] Decisions about the duration of ESY services (i.e., number of weeks, days per week, and hours per day) must also be individualized.[9]

Factors to Consider

What factors must the team consider in deciding if my child will receive ESY services?

The factors that your child's IEP team must consider are usually described in your state special education regulations. As a general rule, the IEP team must decide if your child's progress and gains made during the school year are likely to be threatened if your child does not receive ESY services.[10]

In making eligibility decisions, the team may not rely on one factor. The following factors are used by some (not all) states in making eligibility decisions.

- Regression and recoupment
- Child's progress toward IEP goals and objectives
- Emerging skills/breakthrough opportunities; window of opportunity
- Interfering behavior; behavior problems
- Nature and/or severity of the child's disability
- Special circumstances that interfere with your child's ability to benefit from special education[11]
- Availability of other resources
- Areas of the child's curriculum that need continuous attention
- Child's vocational needs

What is "regression and recoupment?"

Regression refers to the loss of skills during a school break. Recoupment refers to the time it takes to recover these skills. If a child is likely to lose critical skills (regress) during a break, and is not likely to recover (recoup) the lost skills within a reasonable time after the break, the IEP team may decide that the child needs ESY services.

At least one court held that it is not necessary to show actual regression to find that a child is eligible for ESY.[12]

What role does "progress toward IEP goals and objectives" play in ESY decisions?

The team should review your child's progress toward the IEP goals. Will your child's lack of progress toward the IEP goals prevent your child from receiving educational benefit? If the answer is "yes," the school may provide ESY services.

At least one court held that it would be inconsistent to rely on lack of progress as the sole criterion in determining if ESY services are necessary.[13]

My child zones out in class, so it's hard for him to learn and retain what he learns. Should he receive ESY services?

Maybe. This depends on the eligibility criteria adopted by your state. In some states, interfering behaviors (i.e., stereotypic, ritualistic, aggressive, or self-injurious behaviors) are a factor in eligibility decisions.

If these behaviors are targeted by goals in your child's IEP and if the behaviors prevent your child from receiving educational benefit, the team may provide ESY services.[14]

Does my child have to demonstrate that she regressed before she can receive ESY services?

No. If there is no data about regression, the child's need for ESY services may be shown by expert opinion or criteria established by the IEP team. The team should examine several factors.

- Review of child's IEP goals (or objectives or benchmarks, if required)
- Observation and data from child's teachers, therapists, parents, and others who had direct contact with the child before and during breaks in educational programming
- Data and observations regarding the child's performance after long weekends, vacations, and past summer breaks
- Assessments of your child, including pre-test and post-test data
- Curriculum-based assessments, including pre-test and post-test data; and other relevant factors[15]

The team must answer this question: "Does the child need ESY services to receive a free, appropriate public education and to prevent the benefits received during the year from being jeopardized?"

When I requested ESY services for my child, the team said they use a "regression-recoupment" formula, and my daughter did not "regress enough" for ESY.

All children, disabled and nondisabled, regress during long summer breaks. The IEP team must determine if the benefits your child gained during the regular school year will be in jeopardy if she does not receive ESY services.

Some courts have held that parents should not be compelled to watch their child regress before qualifying for ESY services.[16]

How to Request ESY Services

The parent, your child's teacher(s), related service providers, and school administrators can request an IEP meeting to consider your child's need for ESY services.

How can I request ESY services for my child?

Before you request ESY services, get a copy of your state special education regulations. Check the criteria for ESY eligibility in your state.

Review your child's file, focusing on assessments, IEP progress reports, and recommendations from specialists. Do you have evidence that supports your request for ESY services? Do you need additional supporting evidence?

In early spring, write a letter requesting an IEP meeting to discuss your child's need for ESY services. Expect resistance, so you should include time to negotiate. Include evidence that supports your request.

Be sure to make your request early. The IEP team may need additional testing of your child before they make a decision about your child's eligibility for ESY services.

In Summation

In this chapter, you learned that the ESY eligibility criteria in your state depends on your state special education regulations. You learned that the IEP team makes decisions about who is eligible. You learned how to request ESY services and that ESY services must be included in your child's IEP.

In the next chapter you will learn about in-state and out-of-state transfers and what schools are required to do when you transfer to a new school.

Endnotes

1. 34 C.F.R. § 300.106(a)
2. 34 C.F.R. § 300.106(a)
3. 34 C.F.R. § 300.106(a)(3)
4. *Letter to Sims*, 38 IDELR 69, OSEP 2002
5. 34 C.F.R. § 300.106
6. 34 C.F.R. § 300.106(a)(2)
7. 34 C.F.R. § 300.106(a)(3)
8. Commentary in 71 FR at 46582-83
9. 34 C.F.R. § 106(a)(3)(ii)
10. Commentary in 71 FR at 46582
11. *Extended School Year Services: Implementing the Requirements for the Individuals with Disabilities Education Act* published by the Virginia Department of Education (2007), page 7 www.doe.virginia.gov/VDOE/Instuction/Sped/ESYdoc.pdf
12. *M.M. v. School Dist. Of Greenville County*, 303 F.3d 523, 537-538 (4th Cir. 2002)
13. *M.M. v. School Dist. Of Greenville County*, 303 F.3d 523, 537-538 (4th Cir. 2002)
14. *Extended School Year Services: Implementing the Requirements for the Individuals with Disabilities Education Act* published by the Virginia Department of Education (2007), page 7 www.doe.virginia.gov/VDOE/Instuction/Sped/ESYdoc.pdf
15. *Extended School Year Services: Implementing the requirements for the*

Individuals with Disabilities Education Act published by the Virginia Department of Education (2007), page 16 www.doe.virginia.gov/VDOE/Instuction/Sped/ESYdoc.pdf

16. *Cordrey v. Euckert,* 917 F.2d 1460 (6th Cir. 1990); *Lee v. Thompson*, 80-0418 (D. Hawaii 1983); *Johnson v. Independent Scholl District No. 4*, 921 F.2d 1022, 1027 (10th Cir. 1990)

13 Transfers and Education Records

- In-State and Out-of-State Transfers
- Education Records
- Selecting the Right School

In this chapter, you will learn what to expect when your child transfers to a new school.

You will learn about in-state and out-of-state transfers and the requirements to provide services that are comparable to those in the current IEP. You will learn that the new or receiving school must obtain your child's education records promptly.

Your child's current IEP describes the special education services, related services, and supplementary aids and services that the school agreed to provide. This IEP provides your child with a free, appropriate public education.

When you move to a new school district – in the same state or in a different state – the receiving school must provide services that are comparable to the services in your child's current IEP.

In-State and Out-of-State Transfers

We are moving to a new school in the same state during the school year. Does the new school have to implement our child's current IEP?

Yes. When your child enrolls in a new school during the school year, she will have an IEP from her previous school. In consultation with her parents, the receiving school must provide services that are comparable to those described in her current IEP.[1]

We moved to a new district in the same state during the school year. The school says they have to evaluate my child, determine if he is eligible, and develop a new IEP before they can provide any special education services. This will take months! Is this correct?

Absolutely not! Your child was found eligible for special education services by another district in your state. That district developed an IEP that provides a free, appropriate public education.

The law requires the receiving school district to provide your child with services comparable to those in the previous IEP. This requirement to provide services continues until the receiving district either adopts the previous IEP or consults with you to develop and implement a new IEP.

We are moving to another state. Is the new school required to implement our child's current IEP?

Yes. When your child transfers to a new school in another state, she will have the IEP from her previous school. In consultation with her parents, the new school must provide her with a free, appropriate public education. The school must continue to provide comparable services until they conduct an evaluation and develop and implement a new IEP for her.[2]

You say the receiving school must provide "comparable services" to students who transfer. What does "comparable services" mean?

Comparable services means services that are "similar" or "equivalent."[3]

> **Advocate's TIP**
>
> Before you move to a new state, get the state's special education regulations, guidelines, and policies. If you visit the web site of the State Department of Education, you are likely to find more helpful information that will help your family adjust to your new school and community.

In a staff meeting our principal said, "We have a 90 day reprieve before we have to look at a transfer student's IEP." Is this right?

No! When a child transfers during the school year, the receiving school must provide services comparable to the services in the child's IEP **without delay**. There is no provision in the law to wait one day, one month, or 90 days to provide these services.

Think about it. If a receiving school could delay providing the services in the child's IEP for 90 days or more, this would deprive the child of a free, appropriate public education for months. That is not what the law intends or allows!

A child with an IEP transferred into my class from another city in our state. How long does our district have to implement the IEP? How long before we are required to evaluate the student and write a new IEP?

The short answer is that the receiving school must implement the child's present IEP without delay. The law does not require a school district in the same state to complete new evaluations on a child with an IEP who transfers.

If a child with a disability transfers and has an IEP from a school in another state, the receiving school must provide the child with a free, appropriate public education. This includes services that are comparable to those in the previous IEP, in consultation with the child's parents, until the district evaluates the child (if necessary) and develops a new IEP.[4]

A child with autism transferred to our school. This child has a "Cadillac IEP" with one-to-one speech therapy and 40+ hours of ABA therapy a week. We are not prepared to provide these services. Can we require the child to stay home, without special education services, until our staff can develop a new IEP?

No. When a child with an IEP transfers to a new school, the receiving school, in consultation with the child's parents, must provide the child with special education and related services that are comparable to those in the previous IEP.

The requirement to provide comparable services continues until the receiving school evaluates the child and develops and implements a new IEP.[5]

Advocate's TIP

Is your child's Individualized Education Program (IEP) current? If a new IEP will be completed around the time you plan to move, ask the IEP team to meet earlier to write the new IEP. A current IEP will facilitate your child's adjustment to the new school.

Be sure to schedule the IEP meeting at least 6 weeks before your move. You want to have time to finalize the IEP and have copies of the new IEP ready for the new school.

A child received special education and related services under an IEP from a neighboring school district. That child

moved to our district. What are our responsibilities?

Your school, in consultation with the child's parents, must provide the child with a free, appropriate public education. Your district must continue to provide comparable services until the district adopts the IEP from the sending district, or develops and implements a new IEP.[6]

Education Records

We plan to move this year. Our daughter will change schools. What steps can we take now to make the process go smoothly?

Good question! You are planning ahead. When your child transfers, the receiving school is required to obtain your child's education records promptly.[7]

Education records include IEPs, evaluations, supporting documents, and other records about special education and related services.

But when you deal with bureaucracies, things do not always go according to plan.

Request a complete copy of your child's education records before you move. If the receiving school does not obtain your child's education records promptly, you can provide copies of essential documents from your records.

When you provide documents from your child's file, always make copies. Never relinquish the originals.

We thought we had all our child's education records. After the move, we discovered that we do not have some documents. Can the new school request the missing documents?

Yes, they can. The receiving school should request your child's education records immediately. The "new school shall take steps to promptly obtain the child's records, including the IEP and supporting documents and any other records relating to the provision of special education and related services to the child ….[8]

Advocate's TIP

Before you move, ask your child's teacher to write a letter of introduction to your child's new teacher(s). Ask the teacher to describe your child, his strengths and weaknesses, and effective strategies for working with him. The information in the letter will allow the new teachers to implement effective strategies right away. Make this request several weeks before you move so the teacher has time to write a thoughtful letter.

A child transferred to our school from another state. The parents report that their child has a disability and an IEP. The parents do not have any education records or a copy of the IEP. How can we provide comparable services if we don't have a copy of the IEP?

The receiving school must take steps to obtain the child's education records promptly, including the IEP, evaluations, and supporting documents.

If the school cannot obtain the IEP from the sending school or the parent, the school is not required to provide services to the child.[9] The school must place the child in regular education classes, and evaluate the child to determine what services the child needs to receive a free, appropriate public education.

Advocate's TIP

Up-to-Date Medical Records

If your child is seeing medical or mental health specialists, get a complete copy of the medical records from the doctors. Get copies of dental records, too.

Selecting the Right School

If you are moving to a new community, you need reliable information about the schools you are considering. These web sites will help.

Great Schools

www.greatschools.com

Great Schools is an independent, non-profit organization that provides parents with information and tools to choose schools and support their children's education.

Great Schools has information about public schools, private schools, charter schools, home schools, No Child Left Behind, and school choice options.

"Guide to Choosing the Right School"

www.greatschools.net/school-choice/

The articles on this site will help you make wise decisions about a school in a new community.

On Great Schools, you can compare different schools in a county or city, prepare for a school visit, and more.

School Matters

www.schoolmatters.com

School Matters is a site where parents, educators and others can view performance, spending, and demographic information for schools and school districts in any state.

School Matters can help parents . . .

- Learn about your child's school
- Compare prospective schools before you move
- Select a new school

The "Compare Tool" allows you to compare test scores, class profiles, district financial information, and community demographics.

www.schoolmatters.com/schools.aspx/q/page=cmp

Advocate's TIP

Scan the important documents in your child's education and medical records. Keep the files on a flash or thumb drive in a different place.

For Military Familes and Students

SOAR - Student Online Achievement Resources

www.soarathome.com/

This new web site allows children from military families to compare state academic standards. They can take a free online test to identify gaps in their knowledge when they move to a new state with a different curriculum and testing.

Recommended Resources

Moving to a New Location: Q and A from the National Dissemination Center for Children with Disabilities (NICHCY) is a useful guide.

www.nichcy.org/FamiliesAndCommunity/Pages/Moving.aspx

In Summation

In this chapter you learned what to expect when your child transfers to a new school. You learned that the new or receiving school must provide services that are comparable to the services in the current IEP. You learned that the receiving school must take steps to promptly obtain your child's education records from the previous or sending school.

In the next chapter you will learn what to do when you have a dispute or disagreement with the IEP team. You will learn strategies and tips for resolving disagreements and settling disputes, and how to maintain a positive parent-school relationship.

Endnotes

1. 20 U.S.C. § 1414(d)(2)(C)(i)(I); 34 C.F.R. § 300.323(e)
2. 20 U.S.C. § 1414 (d)(2)(C)(i)(II); 34 C.F.R. § 300.323(f); Commentary in 71 FR at 46681
3. Commentary in 71 FR at 46681
4. 20 U.S.C. § 1414(d)(2)(C); 34 C.F.R. § 300.323
5. 34 C.F.R. § 300.323(f)
6. 34 C.F.R. § 300.323(e)
7. 20 U.S.C. § 1414(d)(2)(C)
8. 20 U.S.C. § 1414(d)(2)(C)(ii)
9. US Department of Education: Building the Legacy IDEA 2004. http://idea.ed.gov/explore/view/p/%2Croot%2Cdynamic%2CQaCorner%2C3%2C

14 Resolving Parent-School Disputes

- Options for Resolving Disputes
- Disputes: Inappropriate or Inadequate Services
- Disputes: Placement
- Relationship Problems

In this chapter, you will learn strategies to resolve parent-school disagreements and disputes. You will learn steps to take if you disagree with the school. You will learn about your options if you are unable to resolve a dispute with the school.

You will learn that conflict between parents and schools is normal and inevitable. Parents want the "best" education for their children. Schools are only required to provide "appropriate" services for children with disabilities.

Economic issues drive conflict, power struggles, and cause adversarial relationships between parents and school officials. Different beliefs, perceptions, and interests fuel the conflict. If conflict is not resolved, it leads to loss of trust, damaged relationships, and emotional and financial stress.

You have two goals: to resolve problems and to maintain healthy working relationships with school personnel. When you protect the parent-school relationship, it is easier to negotiate for special education services and supports.

Options for Resolving Disputes

If you disagree with the IEP team's plan to educate your child, there are several options you can use to resolve the dispute:

- Negotiate and resolve the dispute informally through the IEP process
- Request mediation
- File a complaint with the state department of education
- Request a due process hearing

I attended the first IEP meeting for my child. I don't agree with the school's proposed IEP. What should I do?

You have the right to disagree with the school about your child's needs, appropriate services, educational placements, and other issues.

Before the school can place your child in a special education program for the first time, you must give your informed consent.[1] If you disagree with the school's proposed program, you should not consent to the IEP. To eliminate misunderstandings, always describe your concerns and objections in writing.

You can negotiate, and try to resolve your dispute informally through the IEP process.

Request another IEP meeting to discuss other solutions. Write a "Letter to the Stranger" that describes your child's history and your concerns.[2] Discuss your concerns with the school members of the team. Try to reach an agreement.

The agreement may be temporary.

For example, you and the school may agree to try a program or placement for a specified period of time, and meet a few weeks later to discuss how your child is doing.

My child's IEP states that the school will provide occupational therapy and physical therapy. I learned that the school did not provide any O.T. or P.T. services for several months. When I asked when they would make up the missed services, the team said they did not plan to provide any make-up services. What can I do?

If you have evidence that supports your claim that the school did not provide the O.T. and P.T. services in your child's IEP, you can file a complaint with your state department of education (SEA).

Your state department of education is

responsible for supervising special education programs operated by school districts, and for ensuring that all children with disabilities receive a free, appropriate public education.[3]

Your state must have system to provide parents with information about complaint procedures and to resolve complaints. If a school district fails to provide appropriate services, the state must ensure that the district takes corrective action (i.e., compensatory education, monetary reimbursement).[4]

The state department of education must resolve complaints within 60 calendar days. An extension of that time limit is allowed only under exceptional circumstances.[5]

A complaint must include a statement that the school district violated a legal requirement in IDEA, the facts that support this statement, and your signature and contact information. If you file a complaint on a child's behalf, the complaint must also include:

- The child's name and address
- The name of the child's school
- A description of the problem (the facts)
- A proposed resolution of the problem[6]

You have one year to file a complaint with the state department of education.

Are other options available to resolve disputes?

Yes. If you cannot resolve your dispute informally or by filing a complaint with the state, you can request mediation.[7] You can also request an impartial due process hearing.[8]

What is mediation? How does it work?

Mediation is a voluntary process that allows parties to resolve disputes without litigation. The mediator helps the parties express their views and positions and understand the views and positions of the other party. Before entering into mediation, you need to understand your rights and the law.

For mediation to be successful, the mediator must be qualified and impartial.[9] Mediators should not take sides or positions. A good mediator must know how to facilitate communication. Knowledge of special education law is less important.

Both parties must discuss their views and differences frankly. With help from the mediator, you and the school will try to reach an agreement.

The mediator can act as a facilitator for an IEP meeting. The terms of a mediated agreement can be incorporated into the IEP so the IEP reflects the agreement.[10]

How much does mediation cost?

Parents and school districts do not pay for mediation. The state pays the costs.

If we resolve our dispute through mediation, what happens next?

If you and the school resolve your dispute through mediation, you will execute a legally binding agreement. Both parties will sign the agreement. The written agreement will state that all discussions during mediation are confidential. The written agreement is enforceable in a state or federal district court.[11]

If you and the school cannot resolve your dispute through mediation, information from mediation discussions may not be used or disclosed in a trial. If either party attempts to use confidential disclosures from mediation discussions in court, the case may be dismissed or the judge may issue an adverse ruling.

Do I have to request a due process hearing before mediation?

No. You can request mediation without requesting a due process hearing. The school may offer mediation to resolve a dispute before a due process hearing.

If you cannot resolve the dispute informally, by a complaint to the state, or through mediation, you have the option of requesting a due process hearing.

What is a due process hearing? How does it work?

A due process hearing is a trial. In most cases, due process hearings are formal, contested, adversarial trials. The parties present evidence to an Impartial Hearing Officer or Administrative Law Judge. The Impartial Hearing Officer issues a decision. This decision may be appealed to a state or federal district court.[12]

The law includes many pre-trial procedures and timelines. Before requesting a due process hearing, you should consult with an attorney who has expertise in special education law and litigation.

You or the school may request a due process hearing to resolve disagreements about your child's eligibility for special education services, the adequacy of services, implementation of the IEP, your child's placement, and other issues.

Disputes: Inappropriate or Inadequate Services

My child is not making progress, so I asked for a meeting to review and revise the IEP. The team leader said I consented to the IEP so I have to wait until the next annual meeting before asking that it be changed. Is this true?

No. You can request a meeting to change the IEP at any time. The team must review your child's IEP "periodically, but not less than annually."[13] The history of the IDEA states, "there should be as many meetings a year as a child may need."[14]

If you or your child's teacher believes the IEP should be reviewed and revised to meet his needs, the district must hold a meeting to review and revise his IEP.[15] Be sure to make your request in writing.

We don't expect a child to wear the same size shoes for a year. The fact that you consented to the IEP does not mean you are stuck with it—or that the IEP is appropriate for a full year. The IEP is a dynamic document that can and should be revised when necessary.

My child isn't making progress. How can I get the school to create IEPs with measurable goals?

A parent says, "My child isn't making progress." Your statement is not likely to persuade the IEP team. You need facts to support your position.

Get a comprehensive psycho-educational evaluation of your child by an evaluator in the private sector. Look for an evaluator who has expertise in your child's disability. Make sure your evaluator is willing to attend an IEP meeting to discuss your child's needs, progress, and describe the services that need to be included in the IEP.

After you receive the evaluation and discuss the findings with the evaluator, write a letter to request a meeting to review and revise your child's IEP. Describe your concerns and that these concerns led you to have your child evaluated by a specialist in the private sector. Clearly state what you want the school to provide (i.e., "three 30-minute sessions of one-on-one speech therapy by a licensed speech-language pathologist per week").

During the IEP meeting, restate your concerns and what you want. The evaluator needs to describe your child's strengths, deficits, and how much speech therapy she requires to receive educational benefit.

Your evaluator must use data and facts to help the team members understand the significance of her problems. The team needs current, accurate information about your child's present levels of academic achievement and functional performance before it can develop an IEP with measurable goals that meet her needs for a free, appropriate public education (FAPE).

The goals in my child's IEP have not changed for years. How can I get the IEP team to write goals that are individualized to my child's needs?

The IEP team must identify all your child's needs that result from the disability. The IEP must include your child's present levels of academic achievement and functional performance, measurable goals, and how your child's progress will be measured.

Because your child's IEP goals remained the same, you need to request a meeting to revise the IEP and develop individualized goals based on current data.

Before requesting that meeting, you need to learn how to write SMART IEP goals. After you learn how to write measurable goals, write the letter to request a meeting to revise the IEP. To prepare for the meeeting, write measurable IEP goals for your child.

Advocate's TIP

Before the next IEP meeting, read Chapter 12 about SMART IEPs in ***Wrightslaw: From Emotions to Advocacy, 2nd Edition*** or download the chapter from the Wrightslaw web site at www.wrightslaw.com/bks/feta2/ch12.ieps.pdf

My child has autism. He needs to learn to communicate. The school provides two 30-minute sessions of group speech therapy a week. This is not sufficient. I want additional services from a speech-language pathologist in the private sector. Can I request reimbursement?

You can request reimbursement, but you should expect the school to balk. The school is required to provide the services your child needs for a free, appropriate public education. The school can provide these services directly or they can contract with a public or private agency.

You need to write a letter to the school that describes your concerns (services are not sufficient to teach your child to communicate) and your proposed solution (additional one-on-one speech therapy). This gives the school an opportunity to address your concerns by providing additional speech-language therapy.

Assume the school refuses to provide the requested speech therapy. The first step is to have your child evaluated by a speech-language pathologist in the private sector. Ask the evaluator to describe his needs, the services he requires (type, frequency, duration) and what will happen if he does not receive adequate speech therapy early in life (there is a "window of opportunity" for children to learn to communicate).

After you have the evaluation, write a "Letter to the Stranger"that describes your child's history, problems and needs, your concerns, and what the speech language pathologist says he needs. Explain that you do not agree that group speech therapy sessions are appropriate or sufficient. If the school cannot provide the speech therapy services he needs, you will provide one-on-one sessions, as the evaluator recommended.

Assuming your child makes good progress, you will request that the school reimburse you.

Advocate's TIP

Learn how to write a "Letter to the Stranger" in Chapter 24 of ***Wrightslaw: From Emotions to Advocacy, 2nd Edition***

My 16 year-old needs to learn basic living skills, problem solving, and survival skills before he leaves school. When I asked the IEP team to develop a transition plan that includes these skills, they said they focus on academic skills only. Is this correct?

No. All decisions about transition services must be individualized. If your child needs daily living, problem solving, and survival skills, teaching these skills should be in his transition plan.

For transition services, team members need to think creatively. Transition services can include:

- Independent living and community participation

- Integrated and supported employment
- Vocational education and adult education
- Courses of study, including advanced placement classes, that your child needs to reach the transition goals[16]
- Transitional programs on college campuses or in community-based settings[17]

We had a comprehensive evaluation of our child by a psychologist in the private sector. We provided the evaluation to the IEP team. The team said they "considered" the evaluation but refused to use any information or recommendations from it. Can they do that?

The law does not require the team to accept the findings or implement recommendations from a specialist in the private sector.[18] The law does require the school to respond to your concerns about your child's educational program. The law also requires the IEP team to consider the results of any evaluation you obtain.[19]

What does "consider" mean?

The dictionary defines "consider" as "to think about carefully in order to arrive at a judgment or decision, especially with regard to taking some action."[20]

The federal special education regulations impose an "affirmative obligation" on the school to consider the results of the evaluation.[21] In one case, a federal court ruled that the school's refusal or failure to consider private evaluations submitted by the parents was a serious violation of the law and denied the child's right to a free, appropriate public education.[22]

It's easier to "consider" and reject an evaluation if the evaluator is not present to describe his findings and recommendations. If you get an evaluation from a specialist in the private sector, ask her to attend the meeting to discuss her findings.

If the evaluator is available to describe the child's needs, program, and what will happen if the recommendations are not accepted, it is more likely that the IEP team will accept and use the results.

Disputes: Placement

Placement is a common area of disagreement between parents and schools. Although the law requires the team to make individualized decisions about each child's program and placement, the reality is often different.

School districts set up categorical programs for children with disabilities. In many cases, the child's disability category or "label" is the primary factor considered by the team in making placement decisions.

My child was born deaf. She has cochlear implants, so she can hear. The team wants to place her in a class with deaf children. The teacher uses American Sign Language. We want her

to attend regular education classes with children her age so she learns to communicate by speaking. What can we do?

You need to hold firm on this issue. Reading comprehension scores for high school graduates who are deaf or hearing impaired are below the 4th grade level. On average, children who are deaf or hearing impaired gain only 1.5 years in reading skills between the ages of 8 and 18.[23]

You have learned that the first placement option the team must consider is the regular education classroom in the school your child would attend if not disabled. Your child can hear. She needs to learn to listen and speak. She can be placed in a regular class with supplementary aids and services designed to meet her unique needs.

Put your detective cap on. Why does the team want to place your child in a class with a teacher who cannot teach her to speak? How many teachers of deaf or hard of hearing children does the district employ? What teaching method(s) do these teachers use?

Write a letter to your IEP team, with copies to the director of special education and the superintendent. Describe the problem. State your objections to the proposed placement. Explain what you want and why.

If the school does not respond to your letter, request that they provide Prior Written Notice.

What is Prior Written Notice?

If there is a disagreement about a child's identification, evaluation, or placement, the school must provide the parents with "prior written notice." Prior written notice describes what the school proposes or refuses to do about the identification, evaluation, or educational placement of your child, or providing your child with a free, appropriate public education (FAPE). This term may be easier to understand if you think of it as "written notice."

This notice includes several required components.[24] The notice must:

- Explain what the school proposes or refuses to do and their alternative proposal, if any
- Describe the school's rationale and each evaluation procedure, assessment, record, or report used as the basis of their proposal or refusal
- Describe all other options the IEP team considered and the reasons why the team rejected these options
- Describe any other factors that were relevant to the school's proposed action or refusal to act
- Include a statement that the parents of a child with a disability have protections under procedural safeguards and how the parents can obtain a copy of the procedural safeguards
- Include sources that parents can contact or help in understanding the provisions of prior written notice

The IEP team decided to challenge my child by putting her in regular education classes, with accommodations. She is failing. How can I get her placement changed back into special ed?

You can request a meeting to review and revise your child's IEP. But before you request that meeting, you need answers to several questions.

Why is your child failing regular education classes?

When the team decided to place her in regular education classes, what accommodations did they write in her IEP? Did all her teachers implement these accommodations consistently?

In Chapter 5, you learned that all children with disabilities are entitled to supplementary aids and services so they can be educated in regular education classes with nondisabled children.[25]

What supplementary aids and services did the team agree to provide? Did the school provide these aids and services on a consistent basis?

Supplementary aids and services must be based on peer-reviewed research "to the extent practicable."[26] Are the supplementary aids and services in your child's IEP based on peer-reviewed research?

The IEP team thought your child could handle the demands of regular education. If she is failing because she did not receive the accommodations and/or supplementary aids and services she needed, moving her back into a special education class is not the solution.

I agree with the services in the IEP but do not agree with the proposed placement. When I observed the placement, the teacher had too many students and was overwhelmed. The aide was out on maternity leave. The only opportunity the children had to interact with nondisabled children was at lunch. Even then, the children with disabilities sat at separate tables, not with other kids. How should I handle this?

If you disagree with a proposed placement, you need to put your concerns in writing. Use facts. Describe what you observed.

Be careful about how you describe the overwhelmed teacher. You don't want to alienate a potential ally.

Explain that the placement does not provide your child with any meaningful opportunities to be educated with children who are not disabled. Use your observations to support these concerns.

Request another IEP meeting to discuss your child's placement. Continue to put your concerns in writing. Because you disagree with the proposed placement, the school is required to give you prior written notice.

If you and the school cannot resolve your dispute, you may need to request mediation or a due process hearing.

The IEP team presented an IEP that placed our child in a self-contained class. We did not agree. The speech therapist did not agree. Can the IEP team "vote" for a child's placement, over the objections of her parents and another team member?

An IEP team should not "vote" on decisions about your child's special education program or placement. This is not consistent with the law about parental participation.

Parents and schools should try to negotiate a solution to their disagreements through the IEP process. The IEP meeting is a communication vehicle between the parents and school. IEP meetings allow parents and school staff to make joint informed decisions about your child's IEP.

Parents are equal participants in decisions about their child's special education program and placement. The team must consider the parent's concerns and the information parents provide about their child.

The IEP team should work toward consensus.[27] Consensus does not mean that all team members agree. It is inevitable that members will have different perspectives. If the team cannot reach consensus, the school must provide the parents with prior written notice about what the school proposes or refuses to do.[28]

The IEP team wants to change our child's placement. We do not agree. What can we do?

Ask for another meeting to explore other solutions. Discuss your concerns about the proposed placement. Follow this discussion with a letter that describes your concerns. You want to resolve the dispute and protect the parent-school relationship.

You may be able to find a temporary compromise.

In some cases, parents and school decide to place a child in an interim or temporary placement as part of the evaluation process. They agree upon a time frame to try the plan. They also agree on the evaluation that will be used to monitor a child's progress. They set a date to meet and discuss the outcome of the interim placement.

The information gained during an interim placement can help the team determine if the program and/or placement are appropriate. Because parents and school staff are working together during the trial period, they are more likely to be invested in a successful outcome.[29]

The IEP team wants to place my child in a special school across town. We want him to attend regular classes at our neighborhood school with his siblings. What can I do?

If you cannot resolve your dispute informally, you can request mediation and/or a due process hearing.

Before taking either step, consult with an attorney who has expertise in special education law and litigation. In most cases, a consultation is not expensive, especially when compared to the expense of litigation. A consultation with an attorney will help you find solutions to the current problem, and develop a long-term game plan.

Although it is impossible to predict the outcome of litigation, you will improve your chances if you apply the Rules of Adverse Assumptions.[30]

- Assume a due process hearing will be needed to resolve your dispute.
- Assume you will initiate the due process hearing.
- Assume all school personnel, including friends, will testify against you.
- Assume the school employee you thought would make damaging admissions does not do so.
- Assume the Hearing Officer or Administrative Law Judge doesn't like parents of children with disabilities.
- Assume you cannot testify.

If you assume that you must request a due process hearing to resolve your dispute, you will realize that you need an expert or experts to provide evidence and testimony. Your expert should have evaluated your child and observed his placement and any proposed placements.

At a due process hearing, your expert can testify about the nature of your child's disability, describe the educational program he needs, and explain why he can learn in a regular classroom if the school provides appropriate services and supports, as the law requires.

If you assume you cannot testify, you will create an extensive paper trail. Your paper trail will include polite letters that tell your story and can be used as evidence if a hearing is necessary.

Relationship Problems

Our child has processing problems and speech-language delays. She receives services from a speech-language therapist. Her regular education teacher is often impatient with her. How can we ensure that her teacher understands our child's disability and the impact it has on her ability to learn?

This is a difficult situation. Depending on your relationship, you may want to discuss these problems with your child's speech-language therapist. The therapist may be able to talk with the teacher and share effective teaching strategies for your daughter (i.e., use fewer words, speak more slowly, give clear one-step directions, allow more time for the child to process spoken directions).

Teachers and related service providers should meet regularly to problem solve, plan, and discuss effective teaching strategies. If your child's teachers and service providers communicate and coordinate, this will enhance your child's ability to participate in general education classes.

Advocate's TIP

Dealing with Difficult People

Learn how to deal with Pit Bulls, Know-it-Alls, Conflict Avoiders, Snipers, Complainers, and other difficult people in Chapter 5, "Obstacles to Success" in ***Wrightslaw: From Emotions to Advocacy, 2nd Edition***

In Summation

In this chapter, you learned strategies to resolve parent-school disputes. You learned steps to take if you disagree with the school, and options if you cannot resolve a dispute with the school.

You learned that conflict between parents and schools is normal. You have two goals: to get the special education and related services your child needs and to protect the parent-school relationhip.

Endnotes

1. 20 U.S.C. § 1414(a)(1)(D); 34 C.F.R. § 300.300.
2. Chapter 24, ***Wrightslaw: From Emotions to Advocacy, 2nd Edition***
3. 20 U.S.C. § 1412(a)(11)
4. 34 C.F.R. § 300.151
5. 34 C.F.R. § 300.152
6. 34 C.F.R. § 300.153
7. 20 U.S.C. § 1415(e)
8. 20 U.S.C. § 1415(f)
9. 20 U.S.C. § 1415(e)(2)
10. Commentary in 71 FR at 46695
11. 20 U.S.C. § 1415(e)(2)(F)
12. States have "one -tier" or "two-tier" systems for due process hearings. In a one-tier system, the state department of education conducts the hearing and the losing party can appeal to state or federal court. In a two-tier system, the hearing is conducted by the school district. The losing party must appeal to the state department of education, which will appoint a review officer or review panel. After the review officer or panel issues a decision, the losing party can appeal to state or federal court." ***Wrightslaw: Special Education Law, 2nd Edition***, p. 113
13. 34 C.F.R. § 300.324(b)
14. 121 Cong. Record, S20428-29 (Nov. 19, 1975)
15. Appendix A, Question #20; OSEP Letter at www.ed.gov/policy/speced/guid/idea/letters/2003-3/redact072503iep3q2003.pdf
16. Commentary in 71 FR at 46668
17. 20 U.S.C. § 1401(34); 34 C.F.R. § 300.43
18. 34 C.F.R. § 300.502(c)(1)
19. 34 C.F.R. § 300.502(c); Commentary in 71 FR at 46690
20. Merriam-Webster Dictionary Online. www.merriam-webster.com/dictionary/consider
21. www.wrightslaw.com/idea/comment/46688-46713.reg.501-520.procedures.pdf, p.46690
22. *DiBuo v. Bd. Of Educ. of Worcester County*, slip no. S-01-1311 (Nov. 14, 2001) www.wrightslaw.com/info/test.iee.steedman.htm

23. ***Educational Advocacy for Children Who Are Deaf and Hard of Hearing*** by Leeanne Seaver, MA., www.handsandvoices.org/comcon/articles/edAdvocacy.htm
24. 20 U.S.C. § 1415 (c)(1)
25. 20 U.S.C. § 1401(33); 34 C.F.R. §300.42
26. 34 C.F.R. § 300.320(a)(4)
27. Commentary in 71 FR at 46661
28. Appendix A, Question #9
29. Appendix A, Question #14
30. Chapter 21, ***Wrightslaw: From Emotions to Advocacy, 2nd Edition***

Appendix A. IEP Statutes in IDEA 2004

Individualized Education Programs (20 U.S.C. §1414(d))

Educational Placements (20 U.S.C. §1414(e))

Alternative Means of Meeting Participation (20 U.S.C. §1414(f))

(d) Individualized Education Programs.

(1) Definitions. In this title:

(A) Individualized Education Program.

(i) In General. The term 'individualized education program' or IEP' means a written statement for each child with a disability that is developed, reviewed, and revised in accordance with this section and that includes–

(I) a statement of the child's present levels of academic achievement and functional performance, including–

(aa) how the child's disability affects the child's involvement and progress in the general education curriculum;

(bb) for preschool children, as appropriate, how the disability affects the child's participation in appropriate activities; and

(cc) for children with disabilities who take alternate assessments aligned to alternate achievement standards, a description of benchmarks or short-term objectives;

(II) a statement of measurable annual goals, including academic and functional goals, designed to–

(aa) meet the child's needs that result from the child's disability to enable the child to be involved in and make progress in the general education curriculum; and

(bb) meet each of the child's other educational needs that result from the child's disability;

(III) a description of how the child's progress toward meeting the annual goals described in subclause (II) will be measured and when periodic reports on the progress the child is making toward meeting the annual goals (such as through the use of quarterly or other periodic reports, concurrent with the issuance of report cards) will be provided;

(IV) a statement of the special education and related services and supplementary aids and services, based on peer-reviewed research to the extent practicable, to be provided to the child, or on behalf of the child, and a statement of the program modifications or supports for school personnel that will be provided for the child–

(aa) to advance appropriately toward attaining the annual goals;

(bb) to be involved in and make progress in the general education curriculum in accordance with subclause (I) and to participate in extracurricular and other nonacademic activities; and

(cc) to be educated and participate with other children with disabilities and nondisabled children in the activities described in this subparagraph;

(V) an explanation of the extent, if any, to which the child will not participate with nondisabled children in the regular class and in the activities described in subclause (IV)(cc);

(VI)

(aa) a statement of any individual appropriate accommodations that are necessary to measure the academic achievement and functional performance of the child on State and districtwide assessments consistent with Section 1412(a)(16)(A) of this title; and

(bb) if the IEP Team determines that the child shall take an alternate assessment on a particular State or districtwide assessment of student achievement, a statement of why–

(AA) the child cannot participate in the regular assessment; and

(BB) the particular alternate assessment selected is appropriate for the child;

(VII) the projected date for the beginning of the services and modifications described in subclause (IV), and the anticipated frequency, location, and duration of those services and modifications; and

(VIII) beginning not later than the first IEP to be in effect when the child is 16, and updated annually thereafter–

(aa) appropriate measurable postsecondary goals based upon age appropriate transition assessments related to training, education, employment, and, where appropriate, independent living skills;

(bb) the transition services (including courses of study) needed to assist the child in reaching those goals; and

(cc) beginning not later than 1 year before the child reaches the age of majority under State law, a statement that the child has been informed of the child's rights under this title, if any, that will transfer to the child on reaching the age of majority under Section 1415(m) of this title.

(ii) Rule of Construction. Nothing in this section shall be construed to require –

(I) that additional information be included in a child's IEP beyond what is explicitly required in this section; and

(II) the IEP Team to include information under 1 component of a child's IEP that is already contained under another component of such IEP.

(B) Individualized Education Program Team.

The term 'individualized education program team' or IEP Team' means a group of individuals composed of–

(i) the parents of a child with a disability;

(ii) not less than 1 regular education teacher of such child (if the child is, or may be, participating in the regular education environment);

(iii) not less than 1 special education teacher, or where appropriate, not less than 1 special education provider of such child;

(iv) a representative of the local educational agency who–

(I) is qualified to provide, or supervise the provision of, specially designed instruction to meet the unique needs of children with disabilities;

(II) is knowledgeable about the general education curriculum; and

(III) is knowledgeable about the availability of resources of the local educational agency;

(v) an individual who can interpret the instructional implications of evaluation results, who may be a member of the team described in clauses (ii) through (vi);

(vi) at the discretion of the parent or the agency, other individuals who have knowledge or special expertise regarding the child, including related services personnel as appropriate; and

(vii) whenever appropriate, the child with a disability.

(C) IEP Team Attendance.

(i) Attendance Not Necessary. A member of the IEP Team shall not be required to attend an IEP meeting, in whole or in part, if the parent of a child with a disability and the local educational agency agree that the attendance of such member is not necessary because the member's area of the curriculum or related services is not being modified or discussed in the meeting.

(ii) Excusal. A member of the IEP Team may be excused from attending an IEP meeting, in whole or in part, when the meeting involves a modification to or discussion of the member's area of the curriculum or related services, if–

(I) the parent and the local educational agency consent to the excusal; and

(II) the member submits, in writing to the parent and the IEP Team, input into the development of the IEP prior to the meeting.

(iii) Written Agreement and Consent Required. A parent's agreement under clause (i) and consent under clause (ii) shall be in writing.

(D) IEP Team Transition. In the case of a child who was previously served under part C, an invitation to the initial IEP meeting shall, at the request of the parent, be sent to the part C service coordinator or other representatives of the part C system to assist with the smooth transition of services.

(2) Requirement That Program Be in Effect.

(A) In General. At the beginning of each school year, each local educational agency, State educational agency, or other State agency, as the case may be, shall have in effect, for each child with a disability in the agency's jurisdiction, an individualized education program, as defined in paragraph (1)(A).

(B) Program for Child Aged 3 Through 5. In the case of a child with a disability aged 3 through 5 (or, at the discretion of the State educational agency, a 2-year-old child with a disability who will turn age 3 during the school year), the IEP Team shall consider the individualized family service plan that contains the material described in Section 1436 of this title, and that is developed in accordance with this section, and the individualized family service plan may serve as the IEP of the child if using that plan as the IEP is–

(i) consistent with State policy; and

(ii) agreed to by the agency and the child's parents.

(C) Program for Children Who Transfer School Districts.

(i) In General.

(I) Transfer within the Same State. In the case of a child with a disability who transfers school districts within the same academic year, who enrolls in a new school, and who had an IEP that was in effect in the same State, the local educational agency shall provide such child with a free appropriate public education, including services comparable to those described in the previously held IEP, in consultation with the parents until such time as the local educational agency adopts the previously held IEP or develops, adopts, and implements a new IEP that is consistent with Federal and State law.

(II) Transfer Outside State. In the case of a child with a disability who transfers school districts within the same academic year, who enrolls in a new school, and who had an

IEP that was in effect in another State, the local educational agency shall provide such child with a free appropriate public education, including services comparable to those described in the previously held IEP, in consultation with the parents until such time as the local educational agency conducts an evaluation pursuant to subsection (a)(1), if determined to be necessary by such agency, and develops a new IEP, if appropriate, that is consistent with Federal and State law.

(ii) Transmittal of Records. To facilitate the transition for a child described in clause (i)–

(I) the new school in which the child enrolls shall take reasonable steps to promptly obtain the child's recods, including the IEP and supporting documents and any other records relating to the provision of special education or related services to the child, from the previous school in which the child was enrolled, pursuant to section 99.31(a)(2) of title 34, Code of Federal Regulations; and

(II) the previous school in which the child was enrolled shall take reasonable steps to promptly respond to such request from the new school.

(3) Development of IEP.

(A) In General. In developing each child's IEP, the IEP Team, subject to subparagraph (C), shall consider

(i) the strengths of the child;

(ii) the concerns of the parents for enhancing the education of their child;

(iii) the results of the initial evaluation or most recent evaluation of the child; and

(iv) the academic, developmental, and functional needs of the child.

(B) Consideration of Special Factors.

The IEP Team shall–

(i) in the case of a child whose behavior impedes the child's learning or that of others, consider the use of positive behavioral interventions and supports, and other strategies, to address that behavior;

(ii) in the case of a child with limited English proficiency, consider the language needs of the child as such needs relate to the child's IEP;

(iii) in the case of a child who is blind or visually impaired, provide for instruction in Braille and the use of Braille unless the IEP Team determines, after an evaluation of the child's reading and writing skills, needs, and appropriate reading and writing media (including an evaluation of the child's future needs for instruction in Braille or the use of Braille), that instruction in Braille or the use of Braille is not appropriate for the child;

(iv) consider the communication needs of the child, and in the case of a child who is deaf or hard of hearing, consider the child's language and communication needs, opportunities for direct communications with peers and professional personnel in the child's language and communication mode, academic level, and full range of needs, including opportunities for direct instruction in the child's language and communication mode; and

(v) consider whether the child needs assistive technology devices and services.

(C) Requirement with Respect to Regular Education Teacher. A regular education teacher of the child, as a member of the IEP Team, shall, to the extent appropriate, participate in the development of the IEP of the child, including the determination of appropriate positive behavioral interventions and supports, and other strategies, and the determination of supplementary aids and services, program modifications, and support for school personnel consistent with paragraph (1)(A)(i)(IV).

(D) Agreement. In making changes to a child's IEP after the annual IEP meeting for a school year, the parent of a child with a disability and the local educational agency may agree not to convene an IEP meeting for the purposes of making such changes, and instead may develop a written document to amend or modify the child's current IEP.

(E) Consolidation of IEP Team Meetings. To the extent possible, the local educational agency shall encourage the consolidation of reevaluation meetings for the child and other IEP Team meetings for the child.

(F) Amendments. Changes to the IEP may be made either by the entire IEP Team or, as provided in subparagraph (D), by amending the IEP rather than by redrafting the entire IEP. Upon request, a parent shall be provided with a revised copy of the IEP with the amendments incorporated.

(4) Review and Revision of IEP.

(A) In General. The local educational agency shall ensure that, subject to subparagraph (B), the IEP Team–

(i) reviews the child's IEP periodically, but not less frequently than annually, to determine whether the annual goals for the child are being achieved; and

(ii) revises the IEP as appropriate to address–

(I) any lack of expected progress toward the annual goals and in the general education curriculum, where appropriate;

(II) the results of any reevaluation conducted under this section;

(III) information about the child provided to, or by, the parents, as described in subsection (c)(1)(B);

(IV) the child's anticipated needs; or

(V) other matters.

(B) Requirement with Respect to Regular Education Teacher. A regular education teacher of the child, as a member of the IEP Team, shall, consistent with paragraph (1)(C), participate in the review and revision of the IEP of the child.

(5) Multi-Year IEP Demonstration.

(A) Pilot Program.

(i) Purpose. The purpose of this paragraph is to provide an opportunity for States to allow parents and local educational agencies the opportunity for long-term planning by offering the option of developing a comprehensive multi-year IEP, not to exceed 3 years, that is designed to coincide with the natural transition points for the child.

(ii) Authorization. In order to carry out the purpose of this paragraph, the Secretary is authorized to approve not more than 15 proposals from States to carry out the activity described in clause (i).

(iii) Proposal.

(I) In General. A State desiring to participate in the program under this paragraph shall submit a proposal to the Secretary at such time and in such manner as the Secretary may reasonably require.

(II) Content. The proposal shall include–

(aa) assurances that the development of a multi-year IEP under this paragraph is optional for parents;

(bb) assurances that the parent is required to provide informed consent before a comprehensive multi-year IEP is developed;

(cc) a list of required elements for each multi-year IEP, including–

(AA) measurable goals pursuant to paragraph (1)(A)(i)(II), coinciding with natural transition points for the child, that will enable the child to be involved in and make progress in the general education curriculum and that will meet the child's other needs that result from the child's disability; and

(BB) measurable annual goals for determining progress toward meeting the goals described in subitem (AA); and

(dd) a description of the process for the review and revision of each multi-year IEP, including–

(AA) a review by the IEP Team of the child's multi-year IEP at each of the child's natural transition points;

(BB) in years other than a child's natural transition points, an annual review of the child's IEP to determine the child's current levels of progress and whether the annual goals for the child are being achieved, and a requirement to amend the IEP, as appropriate, to enable the child to continue to meet the measurable goals set out in the IEP;

(CC) if the IEP Team determines on the basis of a review that the child is not making sufficient progress toward the goals described in the multi-year IEP, a requirement that the local educational agency shall ensure that the IEP Team carries out a more thorough review of the IEP in accordance with paragraph (4) within 30 calendar days; and

(DD) at the request of the parent, a requirement that the IEP Team shall conduct a review of the child's multi-year IEP rather than or subsequent to an annual review.

(B) Report. Beginning 2 years after the date of enactment of the Individuals with Disabilities Education Improvement Act of 2004, the Secretary shall submit an annual report to the Committee on Education and the Workforce of the House of Representatives and the Committee on Health, Education, Labor, and Pensions of the Senate regarding the effectiveness of the program under this paragraph and any specific recommendations for broader implementation of such program, including

(i) reducing–

(I) the paperwork burden on teachers, principals, administrators, and related service providers; and

(II) noninstructional time spent by teachers in complying with this part;

(ii) enhancing longer-term educational planning;

(iii) improving positive outcomes for children with disabilities;

(iv) promoting collaboration between IEP Team members; and

(v) ensuring satisfaction of family members.

(C) Definition. In this paragraph, the term 'natural transition points' means those periods that are close in time to the transition of a child with a disability from preschool to elementary grades, from elementary grades to middle or junior high school grades, from middle or junior high school grades to secondary school grades, and from secondary school grades to post-secondary activities, but in no case a period longer than 3 years.

(6) Failure to Meet Transition Objectives. If a participating agency, other than the local educational agency, fails to provide the transition services described in the IEP in accordance with paragraph (1)(A)(i)(VIII), the local educational agency shall reconvene the IEP Team to identify alternative strategies to meet the transition objectives for the child set out in the IEP.

(7) Children with Disabilities in Adult Prisons.

(A) In General. The following requirements shall not apply to children with disabilities who are convicted as adults under State law and incarcerated in adult prisons:

(i) The requirements contained in Section 1412(a)(16) of this title and paragraph (1)(A)(i)(VI) (relating to participation of children with disabilities in general assessments).

(ii) The requirements of items (aa) and (bb) of paragraph (1)(A)(i)(VIII) (relating to transition planning and transition services), do not apply with respect to such children whose eligibility under this part will end, because of such children's age, before such children will be released from prison.

(B) Additional Requirement. If a child with a disability is convicted as an adult under State law and incarcerated in an adult prison, the child's IEP Team may modify the child's IEP or placement notwithstanding the requirements of Sections 1412(a)(5)(A) of this title and paragraph (1)(A) if the State has demonstrated a bona fide security or compelling penological interest that cannot otherwise be accommodated.

(e) Educational Placements. Each local educational agency or State educational agency shall ensure that the parents of each child with a disability are members of any group that makes decisions on the educational placement of their child.

(f) Alternative Means of Meeting Participation. When conducting IEP Team meetings and placement meetings pursuant to this section, Section 1415(e) of this title, and Section 1415(f)(1)(B) of this title, and carrying out administrative matters under Section 1415 of this title (such as scheduling, exchange of witness lists, and status conferences), the parent of a child with a disability and a local educational agency may agree to use alternative means of meeting participation, such as video conferences and conference calls.

END

Appendix B. IEP Regulations, 34 C.F.R Part 300

§300.320 Definition of individualized education program.

§300.321 IEP Team.

§300.322 Parent participation.

§300.323 When IEPs must be in effect.

Development of the IEP

§300.324 Development, review, and revision of IEP.

§300.325 Private school placements by public agencies.

§300.326 [Reserved]

§300.327 Educational placements.

§300.328 Alternative means of meeting participation.

§300.320 Definition of individualized education program.

(a) General. As used in this part, the term individualized education program or IEP means a written statement for each child with a disability that is developed, reviewed, and revised in a meeting in accordance with §§300.320 through 300.324, and that must include--

(1) A statement of the child's present levels of academic achievement and functional performance, including--

(i) How the child's disability affects the child's involvement and progress in the general education curriculum (i.e., the same curriculum as for nondisabled children); or

(ii) For preschool children, as appropriate, how the disability affects the child's participation in appropriate activities;

(2)

(i) A statement of measurable annual goals, including academic and functional goals designed to--

(A) Meet the child's needs that result from the child's disability to enable the child to be involved in and make progress in the general education curriculum; and

(B) Meet each of the child's other educational needs that result from the child's disability;

(ii) For children with disabilities who take alternate assessments aligned to alternate achievement standards, a description of benchmarks or short-term objectives;

(3) A description of--

(i) How the child's progress toward meeting the annual goals described in paragraph (2) of this section will be measured; and

(ii) When periodic reports on the progress the child is making toward meeting the annual goals (such as through the use of quarterly or other periodic reports, concurrent with the issuance of report cards) will be provided;

(4) A statement of the special education and

related services and supplementary aids and services, based on peer-reviewed research to the extent practicable, to be provided to the child, or on behalf of the child, and a statement of the program modifications or supports for school personnel that will be provided to enable the child--

(i) To advance appropriately toward attaining the annual goals;

(ii) To be involved in and make progress in the general education curriculum in accordance with paragraph (a)(1) of this section, and to participate in extracurricular and other non-academic activities; and

(iii) To be educated and participate with other children with disabilities and nondisabled children in the activities described in this section;

(5) An explanation of the extent, if any, to which the child will not participate with non-disabled children in the regular class and in the activities described in paragraph (a)(4) of this section;

(6)

(i) A statement of any individual appropriate accommodations that are necessary to measure the academic achievement and functional performance of the child on State and districtwide assessments consistent with section 612(a)(16) of the Act; and

(ii) If the IEP Team determines that the child must take an alternate assessment instead of a particular regular State or districtwide assessment of student achievement, a statement of **why**--

(A) The child cannot participate in the regular assessment; and

(B) The particular alternate assessment selected is appropriate for the child; and

(7) The projected date for the beginning of the services and modifications described in paragraph (a)(4) of this section, and the anticipated frequency, location, and duration of those services and modifications.

(b) Transition services. Beginning not later than the first IEP to be in effect when the child turns 16, or younger if determined appropriate by the IEP Team, and updated annually, thereafter, the IEP must include--

(1) Appropriate measurable postsecondary goals based upon age appropriate transition assessments related to training, education, employment, and, where appropriate, independent living skills; and

(2) The transition services (including courses of study) needed to assist the child in reaching those goals.

(c) Transfer of rights at age of majority. Beginning not later than one year before the child reaches the age of majority under State law, the IEP must include a statement that the child has been informed of the child's rights under Part B of the Act, if any, that will transfer to the child on reaching the age of majority under §300.520.

(d) Construction. Nothing in this section shall be construed to require--

(1) That additional information be included in a child's IEP beyond what is explicitly required in section 614 of the Act; or

(2) The IEP Team to include information under one component of a child's IEP that is already contained under another component of the child's IEP. (Authority: 20 U.S.C. 1414(d)(1)(A) and (d)(6))

§300.321 IEP Team.

(a) General. The public agency must ensure that the IEP Team for each child with a disability includes-

(1) The parents of the child;

(2) Not less than one regular education teacher of the child (if the child is, or may be, participating in the regular education environment);

(3) Not less than one special education teacher of the child, or where appropriate, not less then one special education provider of the child;

(4) A representative of the public agency who--

(i) Is qualified to provide, or supervise the provision of, specially designed instruction to meet the unique needs of children with disabilities;

(ii) Is knowledgeable about the general education curriculum; and

(iii) Is knowledgeable about the availability of resources of the public agency.

(5) An individual who can interpret the instructional implications of evaluation results, who may be a member of the team described in paragraphs (a)(2) through (a)(6) of this section;

(6) At the discretion of the parent or the agency, other individuals who have knowledge or special expertise regarding the child, including related services personnel as appropriate; and

(7) Whenever appropriate, the child with a disability.

(b) Transition services participants.

(1) In accordance with paragraph (a)(7) of this section, the public agency must invite a child with a disability to attend the child's IEP Team meeting if a purpose of the meeting will be the consideration of the postsecondary goals for the child and the transition services needed to assist the child in reaching those goals under §300.320(b).

(2) If the child does not attend the IEP Team meeting, the public agency must take other steps to ensure that the child's preferences and interests are considered.

(3) To the extent appropriate, with the consent of the parents or a child who has reached the age of majority, in implementing the requirements of paragraph (b)(1) of this section, the public agency must invite a representative of any participating agency that is likely to be responsible for providing or paying for transition services.

(c) Determination of knowledge and special expertise. The determination of the knowledge or special expertise of any individual described in paragraph (a)(6) of this section must be made by the party (parents or public agency) who invited the individual to be a member of the IEP Team.

(d) Designating a public agency representative. A public agency may designate a public agency member of the IEP Team to also serve as the agency representative, if the criteria in paragraph (a)(4) of this section are satisfied.

(e) IEP Team attendance.

(1) A member of the IEP Team described in paragraphs (a)(2) through (a)(5) of this section is not required to attend an IEP Team meeting, in whole or in part, if the parent of a child with a disability and the public agency

agree, in writing, that the attendance of the member is not necessary because the member's area of the curriculum or related services is not being modified or discussed in the meeting.

(2) A member of the IEP Team described in paragraph (e)(1) of this section may be excused from attending an IEP Team meeting, in whole or in part, when the meeting involves a modification to or discussion of the member's area of the curriculum or related services, if--

(i) The parent, in writing, and the public agency consent to the excusal; and

(ii) The member submits, in writing to the parent and the IEP Team, input into the development of the IEP prior to the meeting.

(f) Initial IEP Team meeting for child under Part C. In the case of a child who was previously served under Part C of the Act, an invitation to the initial IEP Team meeting must, at the request of the parent, be sent to the Part C service coordinator or other representatives of the Part C system to assist with the smooth transition of services. (Authority: 20 U.S.C. 1414(d)(1)(B)-(d)(1)(D))

§300.322 Parent participation.

(a) Public agency responsibility - general. Each public agency must take steps to ensure that one or both of the parents of a child with a disability are present at each IEP Team meeting or are afforded the opportunity to participate, including-

(1) Notifying parents of the meeting early enough to ensure that they will have an opportunity to attend; and

(2) Scheduling the meeting at a mutually agreed on time and place.

(b) Information provided to parents.

(1) The notice required under paragraph (a)(1) of this section must--

(i) Indicate the purpose, time, and location of the meeting and who will be in attendance; and

(ii) Inform the parents of the provisions in §300.321(a)(6) and (c) (relating to the participation of other individuals on the IEP Team who have knowledge or special expertise about the child), and §300.321(f) (relating to the participation of the Part C service coordinator or other representatives of the Part C system at the initial IEP Team meeting for a child previously served under Part C of the Act).

(2) For a child with a disability beginning not later than the first IEP to be in effect when the child turns 16, or younger if determined appropriate by the IEP Team, the notice also must--

(i) Indicate--

(A) That a purpose of the meeting will be the consideration of the postsecondary goals and transition services for the child, in accordance with §300.320(b); and

(B) That the agency will invite the student; and

(ii) Identify any other agency that will be invited to send a representative.

(c) Other methods to ensure parent participation. If neither parent can attend an IEP Team meeting, the public agency must use other methods to ensure parent participation, including individual or conference telephone calls, consistent with §300.328 (related to alternative means of meeting participation).

(d) Conducting an IEP Team meeting without a parent in attendance. A meeting may be conducted without a parent in attendance if the public agency is unable to convince the parents that they should attend. In this case, the public agency must keep a record of its attempts to arrange a mutually agreed on time and place, such as--

(1) Detailed records of telephone calls made or attempted and the results of those calls;

(2) Copies of correspondence sent to the parents and any responses received; and

(3) Detailed records of visits made to the parent's home or place of employment and the results of those visits.

(e) Use of interpreters or other action, as appropriate. The public agency must take whatever action is necessary to ensure that the parent understands the proceedings of the IEP Team meeting, including arranging for an interpreter for parents with deafness or whose native language is other than English.

(f) Parent copy of child's IEP. The public agency must give the parent a copy of the child's IEP at no cost to the parent. (Authority: 20 U.S.C. 1414(d)(1)(B)(i))

§300.323 When IEPs must be in effect.

(a) General. At the beginning of each school year, each public agency must have in effect, for each child with a disability within its jurisdiction, an IEP, as defined in §300.320.

(b) IEP or IFSP for children aged three through five.

(1) In the case of a child with a disability aged three through five (or, at the discretion of the SEA, a two-year-old child with a disability who will turn age three during the school year), the IEP Team must consider an IFSP that contains the IFSP content (including the natural environments statement) described in section 636(d) of the Act and its implementing regulations (including an educational component that promotes school readiness and incorporates pre-literacy, language, and numeracy skills for children with IFSPs under this section who are at least three years of age), and that is developed in accordance with the IEP procedures under this part. The IFSP may serve as the IEP of the child, if using the IFSP as the IEP is--

(i) Consistent with State policy; and

(ii) Agreed to by the agency and the child's parents.

(2) In implementing the requirements of paragraph (b)(1) of this section, the public agency must--

(i) Provide to the child's parents a detailed explanation of the differences between an IFSP and an IEP; and

(ii) If the parents choose an IFSP, obtain written informed consent from the parents.

(c) Initial IEPs; provision of services.

Each public agency must ensure that--

(1) A meeting to develop an IEP for a child is conducted within 30 days of a determination that the child needs special education and related services; and

(2) As soon as possible following development of the IEP, special education and related services are made available to the child in accordance with the child's IEP.

(d) Accessibility of child's IEP to teachers and others. Each public agency must ensure that-

(1) The child's IEP is accessible to each regular education teacher, special education teacher, related services provider, and any other service

provider who is responsible for its implementation; and

(2) Each teacher and provider described in paragraph (d)(1) of this section is informed of--

(i) His or her specific responsibilities related to implementing the child's IEP; and

(ii) The specific accommodations, modifications, and supports that must be provided for the child in accordance with the IEP.

(e) IEPs for children who transfer public agencies in the same State. If a child with a disability (who had an IEP that was in effect in a previous public agency in the same State) transfers to a new public agency in the same State, and enrolls in a new school within the same school year, the new public agency (in consultation with the parents) must provide FAPE to the child (including services comparable to those described in the child's IEP from the previous public agency), until the new public agency either--

(1) Adopts the child's IEP from the previous public agency; or

(2) Develops, adopts, and implements a new IEP that meets the applicable requirements in §§300.320 through 300.324.

(f) IEPs for children who transfer from another State. If a child with a disability (who had an IEP that was in effect in a previous public agency in another State) transfers to a public agency in a new State, and enrolls in a new school within the same school year, the new public agency (in consultation with the parents) must provide the child with FAPE (including services comparable to those described in the child's IEP from the previous public agency), until the new public agency--

(1) Conducts an evaluation pursuant to §§300.304 through 300.306 (if determined to be necessary by the new public agency); and

(2) Develops, adopts, and implements a new IEP, if appropriate, that meets the applicable requirements in §§300.320 through 300.324.

(g) Transmittal of records. To facilitate the transition for a child described in paragraphs (e) and (f) of this section--

(1) The new public agency in which the child enrolls must take reasonable steps to promptly obtain the child's records, including the IEP and supporting documents and any other records relating to the provision of special education or related services to the child, from the previous public agency in which the child was enrolled, pursuant to 34 CFR 99.31(a)(2); and

(2) The previous public agency in which the child was enrolled must take reasonable steps to promptly respond to the request from the new public agency. (Authority: 20 U.S.C. 1414(d)(2)(A)-(C))

Development of IEP

§300.324 Development, review, and revision of IEP.

(a) Development of IEP.

(1) General. In developing each child's IEP, the IEP Team must consider--

(i) The strengths of the child;

(ii) The concerns of the parents for enhancing the education of their child;

(iii) The results of the initial or most recent evaluation of the child; and

(iv) The academic, developmental, and functional needs of the child.

(2) Consideration of special factors. The IEP Team must--

(i) In the case of a child whose behavior impedes the child's learning or that of others, consider the use of positive behavioral interventions and supports, and other strategies, to address that behavior;

(ii) In the case of a child with limited English proficiency, consider the language needs of the child as those needs relate to the child's IEP;

(iii) In the case of a child who is blind or visually impaired, provide for instruction in Braille and the use of Braille unless the IEP Team determines, after an evaluation of the child's reading and writing skills, needs, and appropriate reading and writing media (including an evaluation of the child's future needs for instruction in Braille or the use of Braille), that instruction in Braille or the use of Braille is not appropriate for the child;

(iv) Consider the communication needs of the child, and in the case of a child who is deaf or hard of hearing, consider the child's language and communication needs, opportunities for direct communications with peers and professional personnel in the child's language and communication mode, academic level, and full range of needs, including opportunities for direct instruction in the child's language and communication mode; and

(v) Consider whether the child needs assistive technology devices and services.

(3) Requirement with respect to regular education teacher. A regular education teacher of a child with a disability, as a member of the IEP Team, must, to the extent appropriate, participate in the development of the IEP of the child, including the determination of-

(i) Appropriate positive behavioral interventions and supports and other strategies for the child; and

(ii) Supplementary aids and services, program modifications, and support for school personnel consistent with §300.320(a)(4).

(4) Agreement.

(i) In making changes to a child's IEP after the annual IEP Team meeting for a school year, the parent of a child with a disability and the public agency may agree not to convene an IEP Team meeting for the purposes of making those changes, and instead may develop a written document to amend or modify the child's current IEP.

(ii) If changes are made to the child's IEP in accordance with paragraph (a)(4)(i) of this section, the public agency must ensure that the child's IEP Team is informed of those changes.

(5) Consolidation of IEP Team meetings. To the extent possible, the public agency must encourage the consolidation of reevaluation meetings for the child and other IEP Team meetings for the child.

(6) Amendments. Changes to the IEP may be made either by the entire IEP Team at an IEP Team meeting, or as provided in paragraph (a)(4) of this section, by amending the IEP rather than by redrafting the entire IEP. Upon request, a parent must be provided with a revised copy of the IEP with the amendments incorporated.

(b) Review and revision of IEPs.

(1) General. Each public agency must ensure that, subject to paragraphs (b)(2) and (b)(3) of this section, the IEP Team--

(i) Reviews the child's IEP periodically, but not less than annually, to determine whether the annual goals for the child are being achieved; and

(ii) Revises the IEP, as appropriate, to address--

(A) Any lack of expected progress toward the annual goals described in §300.320(a)(2), and in the general education curriculum, if appropriate;

(B) The results of any reevaluation conducted under §300.303;

(C) Information about the child provided to, or by, the parents, as described under §300.305(a)(2);

(D) The child's anticipated needs; or

(E) Other matters.

(2) Consideration of special factors. In conducting a review of the child's IEP, the IEP Team must consider the special factors described in paragraph (a)(2) of this section.

(3) Requirement with respect to regular education teacher. A regular education teacher of the child, as a member of the IEP Team, must, consistent with paragraph (a)(3) of this section, participate in the review and revision of the IEP of the child.

(c) Failure to meet transition objectives.

(1) Participating agency failure. If a participating agency, other than the public agency, fails to provide the transition services described in the IEP in accordance with §300.320(b), the public agency must reconvene the IEP Team to identify alternative strategies to meet the transition objectives for the child set out in the IEP.

(2) Construction. Nothing in this part relieves any participating agency, including a State vocational rehabilitation agency, of the responsibility to provide or pay for any transition service that the agency would otherwise provide to children with disabilities who meet the eligibility criteria of that agency.

(d) Children with disabilities in adult prisons.

(1) Requirements that do not apply. The following requirements do not apply to children with disabilities who are convicted as adults under State law and incarcerated in adult prisons:

(i) The requirements contained in section 612(a)(16) of the Act and §300.320(a)(6) (relating to participation of children with disabilities in general assessments).

(ii) The requirements in §300.320(b) (relating to transition planning and transition services) do not apply with respect to the children whose eligibility under Part B of the Act will end, because of their age, before they will be eligible to be released from prison based on consideration of their sentence and eligibility for early release.

(2) Modifications of IEP or placement.

(i) Subject to paragraph (d)(2)(ii) of this section, the IEP Team of a child with a disability who is convicted as an adult under State law and incarcerated in an adult prison may modify the child's IEP or placement if the State has demonstrated a bona fide security or compelling penological interest that cannot otherwise be accommodated.

(ii) The requirements of §§300.320 (relating to IEPs), and 300.112 (relating to LRE), do not apply with respect to the modifications described in paragraph (d)(2)(i) of this section. (Authority: 20 U.S.C. 1412(a)(1), 1412(a)(12)(A)(i), 1414(d)(3), (4)(B), and (7); and 1414(e))

§300.325 Private school placements by public agencies.

(a) Developing IEPs.

(1) Before a public agency places a child with a disability in, or refers a child to, a private school or facility, the agency must initiate and conduct a meeting to develop an IEP for the child in accordance with §§300.320 and 300.324.

(2) The agency must ensure that a representative of the private school or facility attends the meeting. If the representative cannot attend, the agency must use other methods to ensure participation by the private school or facility, including individual or conference telephone calls.

(b) Reviewing and revising IEPs.

(1) After a child with a disability enters a private school or facility, any meetings to review and revise the child's IEP may be initiated and conducted by the private school or facility at the discretion of the public agency.

(2) If the private school or facility initiates and conducts these meetings, the public agency must ensure that the parents and an agency representative--

(i) Are involved in any decision about the child's IEP; and

(ii) Agree to any proposed changes in the IEP before those changes are implemented.

(c) Responsibility. Even if a private school or facility implements a child's IEP, responsibility for compliance with this part remains with the public agency and the SEA. (Authority: 20 U.S.C. 1412(a)(10)(B))

§300.326 [Reserved]

§300.327 Educational placements.

Consistent with §300.501(c), each public agency must ensure that the **parents** of each child with a disability **are members of any group** that makes decisions on the educational placement of their child. (Authority: 20 U.S.C. 1414(e))

§300.328 Alternative means of meeting participation.

When conducting IEP Team meetings and placement meetings pursuant to this subpart, and subpart E of this part, and carrying out administrative matters under section 615 of the Act (such as scheduling, exchange of witness lists, and status conferences), the parent of a child with a disability and a public agency may agree to use alternative means of meeting participation, such as video conferences and conference calls. (Authority: 20 U.S.C. 1414(f))

END

Appendix C. Glossary of Terms

A

Ability Testing. Use of standardized tests to evaluate an individual's performance in a specific area (i.e., cognitive, psychomotor, or physical functioning).

Achievement tests. Standardized tests that measure knowledge and skills in academic subject areas (i.e., math, spelling, and reading).

Accommodations. Changes in how test is administered that do not substantially alter what the test measures; includes changes in presentation format, response format, test setting or test timing.

Achievement test. Test that measures competency in a particular area of knowledge or skill; measures mastery or acquisition of skills.

Adequate Yearly Progress (AYP). Refers to annual improvement that states, school districts and schools must make each year, as measured by academic assessments, so that all public elementary and secondary schools have the same high academic standards.

Age Equivalent. The chronological age in a population for which a score is the median (middle) score. If children who are 10 years and 6 months old have a median score of 17 on a test, the score 17 has an age equivalent of 10-6.

Alternative assessment. Usually means an alternative to a paper and pencil test; refers to non-conventional methods of assessing achievement (e.g., work samples and portfolios).

Aptitude. An individual's ability to learn or to develop proficiency in an area if provided with appropriate education or training. Aptitude tests include tests of general academic (scholastic) ability; tests of special abilities (i.e., verbal, numerical, mechanical); tests that assess "readiness" for learning; and tests that measure ability and previous learning that are used to predict future performance.

Assessment. The process of testing to measure skills and abilities. Assessments include aptitude tests, achievement tests, and screening tests.

Assistive technology device. Equipment used to maintain or improve the capabilities of a child with a disability.

Audiology. Related service; includes identification, determination of hearing loss, and referral for habilitation of hearing.

Autism. IDEA disability category; refers to a developmental disability that significantly affects verbal and nonverbal communication, social interaction that adversely affects educational performance.

B

Behavior intervention plan. A plan of positive behavioral interventions in the IEP of a child whose behaviors interfere with his/her learning or that of others.

Benchmark. Levels of academic performance used as checkpoints to monitor progress toward performance goals and/or academic standards.

C

C.F.R. Code of Federal Regulations.

Child with a disability. A child with mental retardation, hearing impairments (including deafness), speech or language impairments, visual impairments (including blindness), emotional disturbance, orthopedic impairments, autism, traumatic brain injury, other health impairments, or specific learning disabilities; and who needs special education and related services.

Classroom-based instructional reading assessment. A reading assessment that relies on teacher observation.

Competency tests. Tests that measure proficiency in subject areas like math and English. Some states require that students pass competency tests before graduating.

Consent. Requirement that the parent be fully informed of all information that relates to any action that school wants to take about the child, that parent understands that consent is voluntary and may be revoked at any time. See also Procedural safeguards notice and prior written notice.

Content Standards. Expectations about what the child should know and be able to do in different subjects and grade levels; defines expected student skills and knowledge and what schools should teach.

Core Academic Subjects. English, reading or language arts, mathematics, science, foreign languages, civics and government, economics, arts, history, and geography.

Counseling services. Related service; includes services provided by social workers, psychologists, guidance counselors, or other qualified personnel.

Criterion-Referenced Tests. The individual's performance is compared to an objective or performance standard, not to the performance of other students. Tests determine if skills have been mastered; do not compare a child's performance to that of other children.

Curriculum. Instructional plan of skills, lessons, and objectives on a particular subject; may be authored by a state, textbook publisher. A teacher typically executes this plan.

D

Deaf-blindness. IDEA disability category; includes hearing and visual impairments that cause severe communication, developmental and educational problems that adversely affects educational performance.

Deafness. IDEA disability category; impairment in processing information through hearing that adversely affects educational performance.

Diagnostic Test. A test used to diagnose, analyze or identify specific areas of weakness and strength; to determine the nature of weaknesses or deficiencies; diagnostic achievement tests are used to measure skills.

E

Education records. All records about the student that are maintained by an educational agency or institution; includes instructional materials, teacher's manuals, films, tapes, test materials and protocols.

Educational consultant/diagnostician. An individual who may be familiar with school curriculum and requirements at various grade levels; may or may not have a background in learning disabilities; may conduct educational evaluations.

Emotional disturbance (ED). Disability category under IDEA; includes depression, fears, schizophrenia; adversely affects educational performance.

ESY. Extended school year services.

Essential Components of Reading Instruction. Explicit and systematic instruction in phonemic awareness, phonics, vocabulary development, reading fluency, oral reading skills, and reading comprehension strategies.

Expected Growth. The average change in test scores that occurs for individuals at age or grade levels.

F

FAPE. Free appropriate public education; special education and related services provided in conformity with an IEP; are without charge; and meets standards of the SEA.

FERPA. Family Educational Rights and Privacy Act; statute about confidentiality and access to education records.

Fluency. The capacity to read text accurately and quickly.

G

General curriculum. Curriculum adopted by LEA or SEA for all children from preschool through high school.

Grade equivalents. Test scores that equate a score to a particular grade level. Example: if a child scores at the average of all fifth graders tested, the child would receive a grade equivalent score of 5.0. Use with caution.

H

Hearing impairment. Disability category under IDEA; permanent or fluctuating impairment in hearing that adversely affects educational performance.

Highly Qualified Teacher. Teachers who are certified or licensed by the state and who demonstrate competence in the subject(s) they teach.

I

IDEIA. The Individuals with Disabilities Education Improvement Act of 2004.

IEP. Individualized Education Program.

IFSP. Individualized Family Service Plan.

Inclusion. Practice of educating children with special needs in regular education classrooms in neighborhood schools. See also mainstreaming and least restrictive environment.

Intelligence tests. Tests that measure aptitude or intellectual capacities.

Interpreting services. Related service; includes sign and cued language, transcription services, communication access translation for children who are deaf or hearing impaired.

L

Least restrictive environment (LRE). Refers to requirement to educate special needs children with children who are not disabled to the maximum extent possible.

Limited English Proficient. A child who was not born in the United States or whose native language is not English, or a migratory child whose native language is not English.

M

Mainstreaming. Practice of placing special needs children in regular classrooms for at least a part of the children's educational program. See also least restrictive environment and inclusion.

Mastery Test. A test that determines whether an individual has mastered a unit of instruction or skill; a test that provides information about what an individual knows, not how his or her performance compares to the norm group.

Mediation. Procedural safeguard to resolve disputes between parents and schools; must be voluntary, cannot be used to deny or delay right to a due process hearing; must be conducted by a qualified and impartial mediator who is trained in effective mediation techniques.

Medical services. Related service; includes services provided by a licensed physician to determine a child's medically related disability that results in the child's need for special education and related services.

Mental retardation. Disability category under IDEA; refers to significantly sub-average general intellectual functioning with deficits in adaptive behavior that adversely affects educational performance.

Modifications. Substantial changes in what the student is expected to demonstrate; includes changes in instructional level, content, and performance criteria, may include changes in test form or format; includes alternate assessments.

Multiple disabilities. Disability category under IDEA; concomitant impairments (such as mental retardation-blindness, mental retardation-orthopedic impairment, etc.) that cause such severe educational problems that problems cannot be accommodated in special education programs solely for one of the impairments; does not include deaf-blindness.

N

Native language. Language normally used by the child's parents.

O

OCR. Office of Civil Rights.

Occupational therapy. Related service; includes therapy to remediate fine motor skills.

Orientation and mobility services. Related service; includes services to visually impaired students that enable students to move safely at home, school, and community.

Orthopedic impairment. Disability category under IDEA; orthopedic impairment that adversely affects child's educational performance.

OSEP. Office of Special Education Programs.

Other health impairment. Disability category under IDEA; refers to limited strength, vitality or alertness due to chronic or acute health problems that adversely affects educational performance.

Out-of-Level Testing. Means assessing students in one grade level using versions of tests that were designed for students in other (usually lower) grade levels; may not assess the same content standards at the same levels as are assessed in the grade-level assessment.

P

Paraprofessional. An individual employed in a public school who is supervised by a certified or licensed teacher; includes individuals who work in language instruction educational programs, special education, and migrant education.

Parent. A legal guardian or other person standing in loco parentis, a grandparent or stepparent with whom the child lives, or a person who is legally responsible for the welfare of the child.

Parent counseling and training. Related service; refers to helping parents understand their child's special needs; providing information about child development; helping parents acquire skills to support their child.

Percentiles (percentile ranks). Percentage of scores that fall below a point on a score distribution; for example, a score at the 75th percentile indicates that 75% of students obtained that score or lower.

Performance Standards. Definitions of what a child must do to demonstrate proficiency at specific levels in content standards.

Phonemic Awareness. The ability to hear and identify individual sounds, or phonemes.

Phonics. The relationship between the letters of written language and the sounds of spoken language.

Physical therapy. Related service; includes therapy to remediate gross motor skills.

Proficient. Solid academic performance for the grade, demonstrates competence in subject matter.

Prior written notice. Required written notice to parents when school proposes to initiate or change, or refuses to initiate or change, the identification, evaluation, or educational placement of the child.

Psychological services. Related service; includes administering psychological and educational tests, interpreting test results, interpreting child behavior related to learning.

R

Reading. A complex system of deriving meaning from print that requires all of the following:

The skills and knowledge to understand how phonemes, or speech sounds, are connected to print.

The ability to decode unfamiliar words.

The ability to read fluently.

Sufficient background information and vocabulary to foster reading comprehension.

The development of appropriate active strategies to construct meaning from print.

The development and maintenance of a motivation to read.

Recreation. Related service; includes therapeutic recreation services, recreation programs, and leisure education.

Rehabilitation Act of 1973. Civil rights statute designed to protect individuals with disabilities from discrimination; purposes are to maximize employment, economic self-sufficiency, independence, inclusion and integration into society.

Rehabilitation counseling services. Includes career development, preparation for employment, and vocational rehabilitation services.

Related services. Services that are necessary for child to benefit from special education; includes speech-language pathology and audiology services, psychological services, physical and occupational therapy, recreation, counseling, orientation and mobility services, school health services, social work services, parent counseling and training.

Remediation. Process by which an individual receives instruction and practice in skills that are weak or nonexistent in an effort to develop/strengthen these skills.

S

Scientifically Based Research. Research that applies rigorous, systematic, and objective procedures to obtain reliable, valid knowledge about education activities and programs.

School health services. Related service; services provided by a qualified school nurse or other qualified person.

Screening Reading Assessment. A brief assessment based on scientifically based reading research that is designed to identify children who may be at risk for reading problems or academic failure.

Special education. Specially designed instruction, at no cost to the parents, to meet the unique needs of a child with a disability.

Specific learning disability (SLD). Disability category under IDEA; includes disorders that affect the ability to understand or use spoken or written language; may include difficulties with listening, thinking, speaking, reading, writing, spelling, and doing mathematical calculations.

Speech or language impairment. Disability category under IDEA; includes communication disorders, language impairments, voice impairments that adversely educational performance.

Standardized test. Norm-referenced test that compares child's performance with the performance of a large group of similar children (usually children who are the same age).

Standards. Statements that describe what students are expected to know and do in each grade and subject area; include content standards, performance standards, and benchmarks.

Supplementary aids and services. Aids, services, and supports provided in regular education classes so children with disabilities can be educated with nondisabled children.

T

Transition services. IEP requirement; designed to facilitate movement from school to the workplace or to higher education.

Transportation. Related service about travel; includes specialized equipment (i.e., special or adapted buses, lifts, and ramps) if required to provide special transportation for a child with a disability.

U

U.S.C. United States Code.

V

Visual impairment. Disability category under IDEA; refers to impaired vision that adversely affects educational performance; includes blindness.

Vocabulary. Words that students must know to read effectively.

Bibliography

A Sampling of Supplemental Supports Aids & Services. New Mexico Public Education Department. www.ped.state.nm.us/seo/library/qrtrly.0204.lre.handouts.pdf.

Age Appropriate Transition Assessment Guide. National Secondary Transition Technical Assistance Center. www.nsttac.org/pdf/transition_guide/nsttac_tag.pdf.

Age of Majority: Preparing Your Child for Making Good Choices. (2002) National Center on Secondary Education and Transition (NCSET). www.ncset.org/publications/viewdesc.asp?id=318.

American Federation for the Blind: NIMAS. www.afb.org/Section.asp?SectionID=58&TopicID=255.

Anthony, Tanni, Ed.S. (2004) *Functional Vision Assessment for Children Who are Young and/or Multi-disabled.* http://nationaldb.org/documents/products/conference/2004_topical_workshop/Partial-FVA-document.pdf.

Assistive Technology and the IEP. www.fctd.info/resources/AT_IEP.php.

Bowser, G. & Reed, P. (2000) *Considering Your Child's Need for Assistive Technology.*" www.ldonline.org/article/6246.

Building the Legacy: Training Curriculum on IDEA 2004. National Dissemination Center for Children with Disabilities (NICHCY). www.nichcy.org/laws/idea/pages/buildingthelegacy.aspx.

Communication Fact Sheets for Parents. National Technical Assistance Consortium for Children and Young Adults Who Are Deaf-Blind (NTAC). http://nationaldb.org/NCDBProducts.php?prodID=64.

Contents of the IEP. National Dissemination Center for Children with Disabilities (NICHCY). http://www.nichcy.org/EducateChildren/IEP/Pages/IEPcontents.aspx.

Cooperative Educational Service Agency Number 7, Wisconsin. www.specialed.us/issues-IEPissues/writingiep/WritingIEPs.htm.

Facts on Hand – Related Services. Families and Advocates Partnership for Education (FAPE). www.fape.org/pubs/fape-33.pdf.

Family Guide to Assistive Technology. Parents, Let's Unite for Kids. www.pluk.org/AT1.html.

Functional Behavioral Assessments: Creating Positive Behavior Intervention Plans. The Center for Effective Collaboration and Practice. http://cecp.air.org/fba/default.asp.

Guidelines for the Roles and Responsibilities of the School-Based Speech-Language Pathologist. (2000) American Speech-Language-Hearing Association. www.asha.org/docs/html/GL2000-00053.html.

Hettleman, Kalman R. (2004) *The Road to Nowhere: The Illusion and Broken Promises of Special Education in the Baltimore City and Other Public School Systems.* The Abell Foundation. www.abell.org/pubsitems/ed_road_nowhere_10-04.pdf.

IEP Guide. (2000) U.S. Department of Education. www.ed.gov/parents/needs/speced/iepguide/index.html.

National Association of Special Education Teachers. www.naset.org/760.0.html.

National Institute on Deafness and Other Communication Disorders Information Clearinghouse. http://www.nidcd.nih.gov/health/hearing.

Nelson, Maureen R., MD. ***Pyschosocial Issues.*** Disaboom Online Disability Community. www.disaboom.com/Health/cerebralpalsy/cerebral-palsy-psychosocial-issues.aspx.

OSEP Policy Letter. (2003) U.S. Department of Education, Special Education and Rehabilitative Services. www.ed.gov/policy/speced/guid/idea/letters/2003-3/redact072503iep3q2003.pdf.

OSEP Policy Letter. (2003) U.S. Department of Education, Special Education and Rehabilitative Services. www.ed.gov/policy/speced/guid/idea/letters/2003-2/redact060403iep2q2003.pdf.

OSEP Technical Assistance Center on Positive Behavioral Supports and Interventions. www.pbis.org/about_us/default.aspx.

Questions and Answers on Least Restrictive Environment (LRE) Requirements of the IDEA. U. S. Department of Education, Office of Special Education and Rehabilitative Services. www.wrightslaw.com/info/lre.osers.memo.idea.htm.

Raising Achievement: Alternate Assessments for Students with Disabilities. U.S. Department of Education. www.ed.gov/policy/elsec/guid/raising/alt-assess-long.html.

Raskind, Marshall, Ph.D. ***Consumer Tips for Evaluating Assistive Technology Products.*** www.greatschools.net/LD/assistive-technology/evaluating-consumer-AT-products.gs?content=783.

Reed, Penny, Ph.D. & Lahm, Elizabeth, Ph.D. (2004) ***Assessing the Students' Needs for Assistive Technology (ASNAT) 4th Edition.*** www.wati.org/content/supports/free/pdf/ASNAT4thEditionDec08.pdf.

Seaver, Leeanne. ***Educational Advocacy for Students Who are Deaf or Hard of Hearing.*** Hands and Voices. www.handsandvoices.org/comcon/articles/edAdvocacy.htm.

Special Education Law: Children with Autism Spectrum Disorder. Massachusetts Advocates for Children. www.masslegalservices.org/system/files/Special_Education_Law_Children_with_Autism_Spectrum_Disorder.ppt.

Special Factors the IEP Team Needs to Consider. Nebraska Department of Education, Special Populations Office. http://www.nde.state.ne.us/sped/technicalassist/iepproj/factors/spindex.html.

Stokes, Susan (under contract with CESA 7 and funded by a discretionary grant from the Wisconsin Department of Public Instruction). ***Autism Interventions and Strategies for Success: Developing Expressive Communication Skills for Non-verbal Children With Autism.*** www.specialed.us/autism/nonverbal/non11.htm.

The Learning Media Assessment. Perkins School for the Blind. www.perkins.org/scout/literacy-and-braille/learning-media-assessment.html.

WATI Assessment Package. (2004) Wisconsin Assistive Technology Initiative. www.wati.org/content/supports/free/pdf/WATI%20Assessment.pdf.

What is the National Instructional Materials Accessibility Standard? NIMAS at Cast. http://nimas.cast.org/about/nimas.

Wright, Pam and Peter. (2006) ***Wrightslaw: From Emotions to Advocacy, 2nd Edition.*** www.wrightslaw.com/bks/feta2/feta2.htm.

Wright, Peter W. D., Pamela Wright. (2007) ***Wrightslaw: Special Education Law, 2d Edition.*** www.wrightslaw.com/bks/selaw2/selaw2.htm.

Index

J

L

M

N

O

P

Q

R

U

V